Radio*active* M
For Radio, Stage

Marina Caldarone has t..... ...ctors at most of Britain's leading drama schools. She has been a theatre director since 1984, twelve years of which as Associate Director of Theatre Clwyd and Artistic Director of the Queen's Theatre, Hornchurch, and is a freelance radio drama producer. She is also an acting coach in television, regular lecturer on contemporary theatre, and has co-written *Actions, An Actor's Thesaurus,* with Maggie Lloyd Williams. She is Drama Director of Crying Out Loud, a production company making voice-over CDs for actors.

Marilyn Le Conte is lecturer in radio acting at the Royal Welsh College of Music and Drama, and teaches radio modules at Liverpool Institute for Performing Arts. A Drama and French graduate of Hull University, she also continues to work as an actress and as a dialect consultant in radio, television, film, theatre, opera, business and education. She lives near Cardiff with her husband and two sons.

Also available

By Chrys Salt

Making Acting Work

The Methuen Book of Classical Monologues for Women

The Methuen Book of Classical Monologues for Men

The Methuen Book of Modern Monologues for Women

The Methuen Book of Modern Monologues for Men

The Methuen Book of Contemporary Monologues for Women

The Methuen Book of Contemporary Monologues for Men

Edited by Anne Harvey

Duologues for Young Actors

Monologues for Young Actors

Edited by Marina Caldarone and Marilyn Le Conte

Radio*active* Duologues for Radio, Stage and Screen

Radio*active* Monologues for Women for Radio, Stage and Screen

Radio*active* Monologues for Men
For Radio, Stage and Screen

Edited by

MARINA CALDARONE

and

MARILYN LE CONTE

Methuen Drama

Published by Methuen Drama 2006

Methuen Drama
A & C Black Publishers Limited
38 Soho Square
London W1D 3HB

10 9 8 7 6 5 4 3 2 1

Copyright in this selection and editors' notes © Marina Caldarone and
Marilyn Le Conte, 2006

The editors have asserted their moral rights

A CIP catalogue record for this book is available from the British Library

ISBN 10: 0 413 77579 8

ISBN 13: 978 0 413 77579 5

Typeset by SX Composing DTP, Rayleigh, Essex
Printed and bound in Great Britain by
Bookmarque Ltd, Croydon, Surrey

Contents

MC is grateful to John Collis of the Learning Resources Centre at Rose Bruford College.

MLC is grateful for the help, encouragement and support of the Royal Welsh College of Music and Drama, particularly Judith Agus and Robert Edge, and Teresa Hennessy at the Drama Association of Wales Library. She is no less indebted to Luise Moggridge and Dave Roberts at RWCMD for coming to the rescue on many occasions.

The authors would like to thank their families and loved ones for their forbearance!

This book is dedicated to all our students past and present who have taught us so much, to Nick Boulton for generously tracking down a favourite speech, to Simon Cryer, the microphone magician, and to the lasting memory of James Westaway, a perfect example of a good radio actor.

Introduction

Radio is a unique medium making unique demands of the actor. For the listener the closest similar experience is reading a book, where the individual's imagination is called into play and the depth and vividness of what the listener and reader 'see' is determined by the quality of the writing or the acting. The minute the listener 'sees' the actor, script in hand, all illusion is lost and belief gone. There's a lot of fun to be had out of this medium but, more than in any other, conviction and commitment has to be total. If you cannot 'be it' totally, the listener will not 'see' you.

In real life there is a certain vocal messiness to interaction; years ago one could argue that radio acting was characterised by a formality in playing, a middle-class, impediment-free and resonant voice, beautifully spoken. Today, hopefully, such preconceptions are being eroded with a broad movement in favour of 'realness' – with whatever seeming vocal 'faults' or imperfections that contains.

Radio's other great strength is in its opportunities for actors of all shapes, sizes, ethnicity and styles. Released from the tyranny of the unchangeable look, actors often find that radio gives them at last the freedom to be themselves and to be able to express an aspect of the real person inside or, indeed, to be someone who is nothing like them!

There is a greater need than ever for actors to be versatile and none can ignore the employment possibilities of radio, with mainstream BBC outpourings attaining far larger audiences than theatre, and reaching international listeners through the World Service. The corporation commissions more new writing than any other medium outside of Hollywood. Radio drama has been penned the National Theatre of the Airwaves with good reason. Add to this the many independent radio producing companies, the talking book companies, the burgeoning CD-Rom market for actors' voices, the prolific – and lucrative – voice-over business, not to mention the documentary opportunities, and you can see why more actors than ever are looking for voice-over agents.

This is a book for actors, both new and those experienced but who have never got round to radio, students and teachers – and the material works equally well for TV and theatre practice. It will help you to prepare for audition and as a training tool. It is also practicable for technical students learning how to turn *sound* into *radio drama* – armed with these texts they can learn how to create sound pictures and learn how radio actors work.

The monologues are largely from contemporary plays – mirroring the mostly contemporary broadcast output. They offer challenging situations that exploit radio's special qualities and demands, giving the actor a chance to create effects and to make emotional contact with the microphone and the listener. They comprise a variety of styles, playing ages, ethnic backgrounds, accents, statuses: some are physically active, others still but intense; some give the actor the chance to create mood with the voice, or to imply unspoken thoughts through the use of an 'inner', more intimate voice.

We hope that you go on to use similar criteria for choosing speeches of your own. A monologue won't work where the character is just talking aimlessly, where there is no emotional shape to the speech in terms of its beginning and ending, where the text requires the actor to shout, where the writing is overly sentimental or trite, or where the speech contains too much complicated action which confuses the listener and makes it hard for the actor to reach the microphone. It will work if there is a 'journey' involving a change in the characters' status, as will finding a speech where there is scope to create a life outside the text. Too much descriptive narrative or overt sentimentality can also bore the listener and tempt the actor to be self-indulgent.

Once you have found a monologue to work on you should look at the context of the speech within the whole play, where available. Your character choices need to be informed, and knowing what immediately precedes your speech – an action or a line of dialogue – helps create your opening objective by giving you an impulse, which is critical. Even if you don't source the play and the exact moment where the monologue fits, make a choice for yourself so that you have a clear reason to start the speech. Also, you may find other extracts within the play that better suit your requirements.

We are not going to take you through how to perform a monologue here – that is up to you, and there are countless books written on the subject. The rules are the same for acting in all its forms. You will have made some basic decisions regarding what the monologue is about, what objectives your character will play, maybe how to go about achieving those objectives. Truth, imagination, commitment and, most important, *connecting*, which is always the best sort of *acting*, are essential ingredients.

Radio*active* Warnings

In radio you have the script in front of you, so it can be difficult to remember to lift the words from the page, not to just read; you might be anticipating your next lines or concentrating on an accent. The result can be actors simply reading aloud mechanically, which is neither truthful nor entertaining. You must commit yourself totally to being in the moment and being engaged in your character's predicament.

Another challenge lies in the lack of rehearsal time; the actor in radio might be tempted to make short cuts emotionally, to generalise. Speeches are usually shorter than in theatre, and the actor may feel the pressure to make an impact in little airtime. It is therefore crucial to make specific choices, to flesh out the inner life of the character sufficiently so that there are no clichés about the acting.

And finally, but most importantly, don't concentrate on *your* voice rather than your character's thoughts as you speak. This can be very tempting, particularly if you do have a conventionally 'beautiful' voice, but it will not sound real, however much you might enjoy it!

We are going to take you through what are the *practical differences* for the actor in this medium.

- **Get the breathing right**. Whatever one is saying – in real life – is informed, breathwise, by what one is doing. We are never doing nothing, even listening, say, to a lecture, has a certain vocal quality. Try this out; think about how the breath is different if you have just walked into a room expecting to see one thing and actually see something else, or if you are having a chat in a nightclub – you may be adrenalised, you might pitch up; the breath always informs the acting and fills in the picture. But remember, it's not all about words on the page; it's also about the spaces between the words, literally so. A terminological plea! The 'pause' *develops* the scene; the 'silence' arrests it. The writer uses these two words for very different effect. Understand, play and enjoy the difference. A pause can be more eloquent than a line of text; a silence more telling than a whole monologue.

- Uniquely in this medium, you are creating the whole picture with your voice, so you have to keep the sound going by not holding your breath when you are not speaking. So, through the pauses and silences **the trick is to keep breathing**, as the saying goes. And the breathing should be audible but not in a manufactured way. The listener can enjoy impulses being vocalised on an in-breath; you're not 'live' only when you have a line, but for every second of the delivery. Equally, you have to conjure the scenery, the costumes, the props, and all with nothing there physically, but everything there imaginatively; it stands to reason if *you* don't see these things, the *listener* won't either.

- The microphone is the person(s) you are speaking to. You will need as much volume as would be required in real life to speak to a person that far from you. So **disengage the diaphragm**. Don't confuse intensity with volume; just talk to the person/microphone, don't project. This is probably the most common mistake made by actors starting in this medium, who are used to having to hit the back row with diaphragmatic support. The general sliding scale is as you build intensity so you decrease volume.

- **Play the microphone**. As you gain confidence with the notion that the person you are speaking to is the microphone, so you will develop a certain fluidity with it; though your feet may stay roughly in the same place during a speech, you could move your body subtly in and out during the monologue, as in real life you might move in closer to say something that is more intimate, or move out as you release a laugh . . . play around with it; confident playing of the microphone makes for a more textured and interesting – and *real* – rendition of the speech. Make eye contact with the microphone, connect.

- **Syntax**. The punctuation, the exact words chosen and the order the words are placed in the sentence are not arbitrary. These are the very signals chosen by the writer to tell you everything you need to know about that character. If we assume that we are how we speak, it becomes crucial to follow to the letter the way your character speaks: that is who they are. The syntax is an exact mirror of the workings of that character's mind; it is their intellect. It might be worth going back to school books to determine what a semicolon means, as opposed to a colon, as opposed to a hyphen; some characters never finish sentences off . . . others talk in short, abrupt full stops. This all means something. Once you unlock the mystery of syntax, it reveals a rich inner seam to be mined by the more discerning actor!

- **Spot**. In radio another person in the studio, known usually as the Spot Studio Manager, creates the sound that would be made by the actor in any other medium, like making a cup of tea, cleaning a window. The radio actor is holding a script so cannot always perform the required activity. Spot creates effects *on the spot* as opposed to those that are ambient and that would be added in the edit. Nevertheless, the actor has to breathe and energise the text as if actually creating the effect. So physicalise the performance. If you are washing a window in the extract, do it with your body and your breath, within the restrictions of holding a script.

Ages: We have stated the ages of the characters in the monologues as indicated by the writers. The ages can be immaterial, for it is the dynamic within the playing of the status that is more eloquent and more interesting. Obviously it has to make sense, but there are characters here whose ages can easily be adjusted by several years without impairing the sense of the words. Similarly, you may well be able to play someone older or younger than yourself, so don't dismiss any speech lightly. Each one offers a different acting challenge, and the creative possibilities are limitless. The joy of this medium is you can change everything about yourself, including age and even gender, although potential employers wouldn't usually want you to play much beyond your natural range, except in small parts to 'double up'. Actors who can convincingly play below eighteen are at a premium.

Accents: It will be obvious to you which speeches are written specifically for a certain accent, and we have indicated this too. If you are going to try an accent it has to be as good as 'native'. You may well get away with an accent onstage that you wouldn't on the radio. The listener is so much closer to your voice, any hesitation or inaccuracy is trebled. However, you could adapt regional colloquialisms so that you can play the character within an accent that works well for you. Be irreverent but authentic.

The Absence of War by David Hare

Andrew Buchan, mid twenties to mid forties, any accent.

This play forms the third part of a trilogy by Hare about British institutions. It documents the nuts and bolts of political life for a Labour Party in seemingly endless opposition.

Andrew, official political minder, total supporter and close friend of opposition leader George Jones, is one of a small coterie of personal aides trusted by the leader. His every waking moment is politics, the norm for so many who choose this profession.

In this soliloquy that opens the play, Andrew is addressing the audience during a re-enactment of the 11 November memorial service at the Cenotaph. The speech sets up the world of the play, a play which tackles the issues around the creation of 'spin' and the new central role of marketing, what the modernisation of the Labour Party actually means and its ethical repercussions.

Andrew I love this moment. The two minutes' silence. It always moves me, year after year. It gives you a breath, just to question. The questions everyone in politics asks. Why these hours? Why these ridiculous schedules? Up and out of our beds at six every day. Read the papers. When you know already what the papers will say. Grab a quick croissant – a croissant! Jesus, I'm from Paisley – then the first meeting of the day. Seven o'clock and I'm there. And outside that meeting, another meeting, already beating, bulging, pressing against the door. Your mind's already on the next one, the one you are already late for, the one which may – God help us – achieve a little bit more than the one you are at now.

What is this for? This madness? To bed at twelve-thirty. After which the phone goes only twice. And once more at three-fifteen. As it happens, a wrong number. But you do not dare turn the thing off.

[*The guns fire again.* **Kendrick** *steps forward and lays his wreath at the bottom of the memorial.* **George** *steps forward and lays his beside it. The* **Liberal Leader** *steps forward and lays his alongside theirs. Then the three men stand a moment, heads bowed.* **Andrew** *looks up.*]

Andrew I have a theory. People of my age, we did not fight in a war. If you fight in a war, you have some sense of personal worth. So now we seek it by keeping busy. We work and hope we will feel we do good.

The Age of Consent by Peter Morris

Timmy, nineteen, any accent.

This play takes the form of two monologues, both dealing with what it is to be a child vulnerable to abuse and what it takes to abuse a child. The other monologue is Stephanie's, a showbiz mother horribly unaware of the damage she is inflicting on her child.

Timmy was put into care at the age of eleven. A tabloid-labelled 'evil child', he had murdered a young boy. He has been successfully rehabilitated, after a fashion, has taken GCSEs and A levels and is about to be let back into society to rebuild his life as an adult. His education has given him the tools with which to think deeply about everyday issues, as this speech demonstrates. During a technology lesson where he is fulfilling his design brief to 'make something beautiful', which for Timmy means a teddy bear, he is recalling a recent acclimatisation trip to the cinema.

The monologue offers a rare and compassionate insight into the mind of a child killer, barely more than a child himself.

Jimmy I'm just thinking.

They took us to see *Toy Story*. The second one, with the lesbo cowgirl.

It was fucking traumatic. I mean, I'm probably making this teddy bear now for some deeply disturbed reason. Really. After I saw *Toy Boy* I started to have these . . . well, not really nightmares, but close enough.

'Cos I was thinking, you know, this isn't Winnie-the-Pooh. It's not about a boy who has his stuffed toys and they're mates, the way mates are, like a pack of fucking lunatics and one's a manic depressive donkey and one's a slag rabbit and one's a fucking pretentious overbearing owl. But at least they're all outside in the woods, getting their exercise, and they're like . . . mates . . .

But *Toy Boy* . . . it's fucking scary, this film. All the toys know they're toys. They know they're not unique. I mean, they have feelings, they can talk and they can think . . . but it's only to learn how to accept the fact that they're just these . . . things . . . like robots . . . these meaningless pieces of shit that can get broken and replaced . . . like slaves. And they don't pretend that it's not scary and miserable and humiliating. I mean, it's just like a two-hour advert for selling the crap toys in the film, but then you watch the toys and they're fucking depressed. And the only other option's getting their arms ripped off, stuffing pulled out, being left on a rubbish heap somewhere, unwanted, some mongy little insignificant thing. (*He gestures with the bear, providing a voice for it.*) Toys are fucking brutal, too, mate.'

But the scene that just . . . I couldn't get it out of my head. The stupid fucking space ranger walks into the shop and there it is . . . a wall of identical toys, all exactly same, all swearing that they're unique and they actually have space ranger powers, and not even turning their heads to see how completely . . . completely the opposite of unique they all really are. Worthless. Worthless is the opposite of unique.

11

And I started having that . . . nightmare, really. Going to . . . I dunno . . .

I guess it was Toys 'Я' Us, I'm not sure, I never have been there.

It was really the shop from the film with a wall of these . . . dolls. Only they weren't dolls. They were me. Or him.

It's like . . . I am totally the same as everyone else out there my age, and totally useless, a meaningless fucking robot, another up-his-own-arse space ranger who can't even fly.

Babies by Jonathan Harvey

**Joe, twenty-four, Liverpudlian, but other accents
would work.**

Babies is a comedy about the collision between the private
and public lives of Joe, and paints an affectionate picture of
a community's fascination for the secrets of those it holds
in high regard.

Joe is a form tutor and learning-support teacher at a
comprehensive in south London, and good at his job. Gay,
but discreet about this part of his life, he's in a long-term
relationship with Woody, also from Liverpool, but there is
much tension in their home caused by Woody's
involvement in the drug scene, mainly marijuana and
ecstasy, to the extent that it's alienating Joe who isn't into
drugs in any way.

Joe loves his work: he's kind, sensitive, and someone the
youngsters find easy to engage with. When the father of one
of his pupils dies, Joe goes to the funeral wake to give
support to the girl and her family, including the girl's
frustrated mother, Viv, from whom he has hidden his
sexual orientation.

Having recently rowed with Woody, he arrives at the
party with the need to let his hair down and soon gets
drunk. He is an instant hit with everybody, including the
widow's gay brother Kenny, who guesses Joe's secret very
quickly. Kenny and Viv argue over him: when Kenny voices
his opinion, Viv is incredulous and asks Joe outright if he's
gay. She takes the news philosophically and leaves him
alone with Kenny who's very attracted to him and who asks
Joe if he's in love with his partner. Despite everything Joe
does truly love Woody and at last he has an opportunity to
talk openly about how he feels, to someone who'll
understand and not judge him. This is a moment of
catharsis for him, and he speaks with absolute honesty.

Joe I love him, but . . . he . . . he fucking kills me (*Beat.*) D'you know how it feels? To stand in a street in broad daylight trying to sort your problems out? To stand outside a pub on a Sunday afternoon and . . . you're talking to him and you know he's off his face, and this big bastard comes up – straight as a die, but he knows he can make his money outa the queens – and he comes up and he says 'Here, Woody' and he hands him a little slip o'paper, the tiniest slip o'paper with a little blue dot on it, and I feel that much of a lowy I pay for it and the big bastard goes away. And then your fella stands there and rips it in two, sticks one bit in his pocket, and the other in his mouth . . . and keeps on talking . . . About us, and the way we are, and the way . . . I make him feel. 'You're hogging me, Joe, I need me mates.' And I just wanna say, 'Can't you wait five minutes? Can't you just wait 'til I've gone and you're back with your mates? Can't you take your acid then?' (*Shakes his head.*) I used to like me, and the way I feel about me. But when you're with someone else it's like . . . it's . . . well it's like you've got a mirror on your shoulder, and what you see in them . . . is how you see yourself. Like it's reflected. And if they're being a twat to you . . . then . . . you think you're a twat yourself, you don't question it. You can't. (*Beat.*) Am I talking shite?

Blood by Lars Norén (translated by Maja Zade)

Luca, early twenties, any accent.

This speech is taken from a modern working of the Oedipus story. Rosa and Eric's son 'disappeared' at the time of the military junta in Chile, in the 1970s, when aged seven. Now, as exiles in Paris, Rosa, an international war reporter, has just written a book about the loss, while Eric works as a psychologist. During the play the three become reunited with horrific consequences.

Luca is the product of an unhappy adoption at the age of eight and is at university in Paris studying to be a doctor. An effortless intellectual, he met Eric as his patient after manifestations of illogical violence. After six months he and Eric became lovers despite the twenty-odd-year age gap. Now, another six months on, theirs is a passionate affair, and Luca is desperate for Eric to leave his wife with whom his relationship is entirely wrapped around the loss of their beloved son. Luca has met Rosa a couple of times. On the last 'chance' meeting, there was a spark of sexual attraction, and he has given her his address. Rosa, who has no idea her husband has been conducting an affair, is a desperate and sexually frustrated woman drawn to this young man who has made his interest clear. She offers herself to him.

The speech comes during this post-coital moment, when Eric unexpectedly lets himself into Luca's flat to see his wife and his lover in a state of undress. Luca is bewildered and angry and lost, while Eric and Rosa soon deduce that Luca is in fact their son.

Luca Well . . . what can we say? (*Short pause.*) What do you usually say in a situation like this . . . You could say it's fucking rude to come bursting in like this without any notice, but that's the risk intruders always run . . . isn't it? But maybe it's just as well. The truth will out, sooner or later. Rather late in this case . . . Honesty is the best policy. (*Laughs.*) I don't know whether I should offer you anything when I've just fucked your wife . . . The three of us have so much in common, it's a shame we have to meet like this, in this dump . . . But I suppose it's like Bourdieu said, forgive me for quoting him, our biggest problem is we've ended up in the wrong place – it's no longer the *condition humaine* but the *position humaine* that tortures us . . . Is it getting cold? (*To* **Rosa**.) Are you cold? Sorry, the concierge drinks, so does her husband, they never go out . . . You know what it's like. There's probably no point in talking about it; it would take so long – betrayal, bad conscience, filth, repetition, acceptance. It's happened now. You'd be better off joining the family therapy centre or doing something for heroin addicts from North Africa.

Bone by John Donnelly

Jamie, early twenties, any accent.

This is one of three characters' interwoven monologues that make the play. It is continuous thought spoken directly to the audience, intimately. Stephen wants his ex to realise he's got what it takes; Helen wants her dead husband back, and Jamie just wants a girl to see him off to war: three lives stripped to the bone.

Jamie is leaving Britain to fight as part of the armed forces. A passionate storyteller, here he is describing part of his last night out with his mates. A seemingly straight-forward guy, albeit a guy with a highly charged sex drive, he is the product of a fairly dysfunctional family – an alcoholic mother and absent father – and he has taken it upon himself to care for his younger sister. Believing he has let her down when she was recently raped and he wasn't there to protect her, he is seething with rage, racism and bigotry. His biggest issue centres on missing his dad – useless as he was, he misses him still.

This extract comprises two speeches from the original text.

Okay. I admit it. I'm a ladies' man. Twelve pints in me, and I could still satisfy two ladies at the same time. Captain Quim they call me, the Quimmaster General, Dr Quim Medicine Woman, Russell Crowe: Master and Quimmander. I am Lord of the Quim. Seriously though, think I might be one o' them sex addicts. It's a medical condition – celebrities get it (well), between you and me, I think they just can't keep it in their pants, but you know these doctors. Any old half-baked bollocks, before you know it, they'll have you up on a couch crying how you was touched up by the dodgy uncle you never had. But me, I ain't got no issues, I'm just hungry for the minge, insatiable appetite, and yes, like Scott of the Antarctic, on occasion I have been known to make the long voyage south.

[. . .]

Ten to eight, place is crawling with trim. Marks out of ten? I'd give her one. We all laugh. Then Mickey pipes up. 'Ere, mate, she looks a bit like your sister! A hush descends. Quick as a flash, I'm there. He's apologising before I even touch him, knows he's bang out of line – sorry, mate, sorry, didn't think, he says. Hands round his throat, you what you what you fucking what did you say? I don't think he meant anything by it, mate, easy. That's Alex – good-looking bastard, swarthy, gets his share. I let go. Don't want to spoil the occasion. I know you didn't mean anything, mate, just a bit sensitive that's all. No, no, no, he says. Not after what your sister been through. 'Ere, this one's on us. Two doormen appear, big bastards, obviously seen the fracas – everything all right, lads? Yeah, lads' night out, says Alex, bit of fun between mates, that's all (you got to hand it to him). Special occasion? the taller one says. As a matter of fact it is, says Terry, with (I don't mind saying) a hint of pride. This lad's off in the morning fight for his country. Turns out taller one's seen active service with the paddies. Any advice? I say. yeah, he says, don't get shot.

Borderline by Hanif Kureishi

Haroon, eighteen, London Asian.

Borderline examines the sense of belonging among the British Asian community of west London.

Haroon is talking to Amina, his now ex-girlfriend, in a dingy car park, where he has been finishing with her. Together for eighteen months, it has been a clandestine relationship – Amina is from a strict Pakistani family who expect her to have an arranged marriage. He is trying to explain who he is and what motivates him. His argument to this point has been that he has to get away, education is his ticket out and that he cannot change the racial bigotry that exists in their society without changing it from the inside and from a position of power. Change from the outside, separatism, cannot work. Haroon, who is also a budding novelist, will be leaving for university in a few months to study law, and rather than putting this separation off until then, he has terminated the relationship now in order to give them time to become friends again before he goes away. Well, that's what he would like.

Haroon You know, when we were kids, my brother and I were taken to people's houses. Dressed up and everything. Like being wrapped in brown paper. We just about creaked. In the houses we visit everything's on exhibition: furniture, their wife's hair, their kids, their kids' teeth. You've got to admire everything. They have to admire you, your teeth, hair, shoes. Everything seems to smell of perfume. You can't touch anything. My brother says he has to piss. He's in their hall. I know he's going through their pockets in the hall. I know he's opening their handbags. They're asking me how I'm doing at school. I'm saying I'm doing well. I can hear fivers settling in his pocket. I can hear my father saying, 'Answer them, Haroon, they're our friends.' I can hear myself saying, 'I'm good at English.' That Sunday he steals a car. It's a Jag. I'm lying on the backseat. We're on the bypass. We're doing sixty. We're doing ninety. We're going out to Greenford. I'm completely numb. They're in a house in Greenford. I'm outside. I can hear him and his friends moving across thick carpets, unplugging speakers, lifting down TV sets. I'm looking out. Soon I'm not looking out. In fact I'm running away. I'm away. They're walking down the drive with a spin-dryer. I'm not there. Two men are running towards them. They're arresting them. My father's cursing. My mother's hysterical. I'm locked in my room. I'm studying, I'm protected, I'm the special son, the hope, my brain's burning . . . (*Pause.*) Everyone round here's too busy serving kebabs and learning karate! No one round here knows fuck all about what you want to know about.

[**Amina**   At least we protect each other here.]

Haroon We've got to engage in the political process. Not just put out fires when they start them.

The Bullet by Joe Penhall

Mike, late twenties, from south-east England, but any accent would work.

The Bullet portrays a family in schism and eloquently observes how squabbling relations often share similar personality traits.

At the heart of the family is Mike's father, Charles, an angry and cantankerous man in his fifties who has recently been made redundant; he believes he's being victimised, but the truth is probably that he's an argumentative bully who rubs people up the wrong way. He invariably takes his tensions and resentments home to his long-suffering wife.

Black sheep Mike inexplicably left home five years earlier and lives rough. He's an alcoholic and a cynic like his father. Despite his apparent self-exile, he's been secretly letting himself into the house, stealing food and money. His mother knows this but has told no one. Thus Mike is able to make this grand gesture of defiance, yet still remain dependent on his family, caring little for the effect his behaviour has on his loved ones, also like his father.

Robbie, Mike's brother, and his girlfriend Carla have arrived home from Singapore for a visit. Robbie is also unemployed but pretends he's in a high-flying IT job. Hearing the commotion of raised voices, curious to see what's going on, Mike has let himself in at 5 a.m.

Later the same morning, Mike is talking to Carla, a rather sorted young woman whose own background is utterly different and who is left reeling by this family's inability to communicate. They are alone. Carla is attractive and sympathetic. It would feel good to have someone listen and not judge. He's told this story before, and it usually does the trick. The 'girlfriend' was actually just some promiscuous girl he once knew. The apparent hesitations are more his attempt to gain thinking time than an inability to speak.

Mike She was my first serious girlfriend. She was . . . the love of my life. You remind me of her. A lot of girls remind me of her. You always see the dead in the living.

[Carla I'm so sorry . . .]

Mike That's how I lost my job as teaboy. See, I was in my room one day, in my room upstairs, and her mum phoned and she said she'd . . . she was coming back from the seaside and on the way there'd been some kind of accident. Yes . . . a Dover-bound juggernaut. She was with this boy, this old boyfriend, the one she had before me and they'd been drinking. Apparently. They'd been . . . they'd been seeing each other again. I . . . I went to the hospital and I sat by her bedside in the hospital, watching as a . . . a large, dark blotch over one eye spread to the other and the lights went out. I watched as the . . . the lights went out . . . and I'd . . . I was holding her hand and saying to her to . . . you know . . . live. Because I couldn't believe this was happening. But she couldn't. Couldn't hang on . . . not even for me.

Pause.

After that I wasn't very good at . . . I wasn't much good at anything. I tried to talk to people about it. I talked to all sorts of people. Strangers. In pubs. I tried to talk to Mum. I tried to talk to Dad but . . . You know I think he thought it was my fault. I think he thought I was just being a troublemaker. Robbie was busy with his university friends and . . . I don't resent them. I just get a bit angry sometimes. To think she could go like that and nobody . . . even seemed to notice. And I just thought . . . I still think . . . it's fucking nonsense – life's too short . . .

Pause.

Sometimes . . . some days . . . I see her . . . everywhere I look.

Silence. He stares into space.

Well. It's nearly eleven. Time for a drink. Lend us a fiver?

23

Crazy Gary's Mobile Disco by Gary Owen

Gary, twenties/thirties, Welsh accent.

Saturday night, small-town Wales, only one pub, one party and three lads in this tragically funny trio of interconnected monologues.

This is from the opening monologue of the play and sets up the war zone that is Gary's life. He has been running the disco at the Boar's Head for years. It is a local tradition. Not any more. And Gary is not happy. In fact the whole piece is about his wreaking vengeance. Gary can be violent and a danger to himself as well as anyone who dares inadvertently to touch him at the bar. He is full of rage and malice. He is without friends and fell out with an only brother, who 'had to leave town' as a result. In Gary's world he is the good man who prides himself on the ability to look after himself and any woman he fancies taking home that night. He has a sense of honour and self-righteousness and truly believes his is the right path – only the world is full of people who try to do him wrong.

Gary Right. Fuck it. I'm gonna fucking spoil it for you all. I'm gonna tell you how this story ends right now.

When I was growing up there was all this – nuclear paranoia shit. All this – 'If the air-raid warning came what would you do, if you only had three minutes to live?'

If I only had three minutes left to live, I'd carry on just as I am. Because in three minutes' time, I'm gonna be fucking . . . in heaven. I'm gonna be fucking the fittest chick in the whole wide bastard world.

So sod all that 'will he get her, won't he get her' bullshit – I'm telling you now, this all ends with me pulling the perfect girl. (*Goes to dial, then thinks better of it.*)

I didn't have anything to do till a crucial business appointment at ten, so I flicked on *Crimewatch* and occupied myself giving detailed descriptions of people I hate to detectives working this harrowing multiple murder case.

Half-nine I have to give it up. I've provided Her Majesty's thickest with a hundred and forty-two invaluable new leads and they're getting a bit suspicious – my voice is . . . kind of familiar from somewhere. It's a real bastard – there's so many people you hate but, like old Nick says, only really a couple of multiple murderers on the go at any one time.

So I fuck off out the house and head down the Boar's Head, where a very different kind of crime is taking place. It's not a straightforward breaking of the law of the land. It's not a crime against humanity. It's much worse than that.

It's a crime . . . against disco.

Thursday night, down the Boar's Head, is disco night. Every fucker knows that. Every fucker, it seems, except Brian the bitch of a landlord, who has decided to replace the disco with . . . kara-fuckin-oke. Kara-fuckin-oke run by a ginger-haired twat with big red plastic glasses and a big floppy red bow-tie.

I cannot; I will not allow my people to suffer like this.

Digging for Fire by Declan Hughes

Brendan, thirties, Dublin accent.

Brendan has organised the reunion of a small clique of friends from university days, including his wife Clare, whose feelings of stagnation contrast with his own steady approach to life. During the course of a drunken weekend, previous opinions of each other undergo profound and irreversible changes when hearts are opened unwisely and secrets exposed.

Clare has confessed to her husband that she had an affair with one of the party, Danny, two years before, and that seeing him again has made her realise she is not content with the status quo of their marriage nor her own lack of direction, and that she is in love with Danny, although it is not reciprocated. The pair have a blistering row, only halted by the arrival of the others, including Danny, from the pub.

Desperate to keep her, Brendan has resolved to forgive Clare and repair their failing relationship. But, as everyone proceeds to drink more and more, all caution is abandoned. Brendan discovers that the whole group have been aware of the 'secret' affair for two years; this destroys all illusions of friendship and his role as the core member of the group.

It's now the following morning. The others are nursing hangovers when Brendan returns from a lone walk. He's been rehearsing what he wants to say – he too has been harbouring secrets to protect others, but no longer. Outraged at the deception of his friends, and in a surprising abandonment of his usual laid back and gentle nature, Brendan tears into the rest of the group, deploring their dishonesty and disloyalty, and shattering all hope of the continuation of their many-sided relationship.

Brendan Well you can shut up for a start, you little shit. (*Pause.*) It's so strange – looking 'round, seeing all these faces I thought I knew, and realising I don't really know them at all.

[**Clare** Brendan, be careful, please. Be very careful.

Brendan Careful how, Clare, do you mean *discreet*? Do you mean smirks and jokes and knowing looks at the big fool's expense? Or do you mean full of cares, bursting into tears in public when the little shit you're actually in love with doesn't want to know? Guess you must mean discretion, 'cause that's what my old friends are expert at.]

My good, old friends. I've been out walking, I must've walked for miles, and I've had just the one thought to keep me company – the thought of my friends, who wouldn't even see each other if it wasn't for me, whom I've met at airports and moved to flats when I was the only one with a car, whom I've lent money to and pretended to forget when it was due back and genuinely didn't mind, was glad to do it – my good, old friends, so discreet that not one of you had the *guts*, or the decency, to tell me that my wife had an affair two and a half years ago with this little shithead here. Not one of you. And you all knew.

[**Rory** (Oh my goodness.)

Clare Brendan, what do you think you're *doing*?]

Brendan I'm rounding things up, Clare. You know, the way I usually do, with a sentimental speech about what great friends we all are. And everyone thinks, what a big fool, and laughs behind their hands. Well, I'm not going to play the fool any more.

Divine Right by Peter Whelan

Greg, thirties, any accent.

The divine right in question is that afforded the British royal family to rule. Set in the year 2000, this epic state-of-the-nation play examines the debate over the future of the monarchy in twenty-first-century Britain.

The Prince, the heir apparent, whose father has just abdicated his right to the throne, has been travelling the country, incognito, to get the measure of his people; he is also on the brink of relinquishing his 'divine right' to inherit the kingship. In a newish but already deteriorating shopping mall in a nondescript town centre, Greg joins him on a bench. Greg is the archetypal working-class boy made good. He is expensively but casually dressed and has that insistent way of engaging strangers in conversation that compels the listener to be complicit in response. This is the first time they have met.

Greg I flew in from Malaga yesterday. No spot on earth like Malaga. Been living down there five years now. Really ace! There's only one word for it and that's 'ambience'. It is ambient. Everything about it is ambient. (*Thinks about this.*) And the talent! (*Does a nudge-nudge expression.*) First day I got there to look at some villa they were shooting a movie along the coast . . . a whole squadron of Moroccan cavalry with turbans and lances and pennants fluttering. Horse's heads tossing . . . all drawn up along by the deep blue sea. Some 'Casablanca' type movie.

[**Prince** Straight up?

Greg No really.]

And all the British ex-pats down there had come out of their villas to watch. Every villain and law-breaker you could imagine! Chestfuls of grey hair. Accents like yours. Bimbo on each tattooed arm. I thought: this is where they got to! These are the Brits who got away. Did it . . . got it and left. These are the Brits who come up from below . . . from the streets. No education . . . which is the secret. If you get educated all that happens is you end up working for those with money . . . instead of having money. The trick in life is to go from where there's no money . . . round the educated classes to where those with the money are . . . and lift some of it off them. Like, in a way, I did. (*He hastens to correct any wrong impression.*) I mean I had to work for it . . . *but* . . . I mean *but*. I drop out of school straight into a sleepy little family estate agents. Didn't take me long to realise what the concept should be. What the boss thought he was doing was selling houses. What I realised was that you should be selling them the *idea* of moving. It's in the mind! It's aspirations! And I could sell that. You got a home?

[**Prince** Not of my own . . .]

Greg Still at mum and dad's?

[*The* **Prince** *nods, warily.*]

So what I would be selling you is the aspiration of the young independent spirit . . . not just a home, right?

[**Prince** Right.]

Greg So I revamp the agency. Rewrite the ads. I create a new image and the boss makes me a partner at twenty-one! It's the housing boom. We make money! Then along comes one of the biggest national building societies, now turned into a bank, the Town and Country . . . and buys us . . . as part of a chain. With that and a property deal I, son of a hardware salesman, am a millionaire at twenty-five. You like that story?

[**Prince** It's a good story . . . yes.]

Greg And the joke is that after they bought us came the crash. Plus they didn't know how to run a local agency. They bought the goodwill . . . but the goodwill was us. The goodwill was me. And they let me get away to Malaga. Become an ex-pat . . . I just come back now and then to see my mum . . . she won't move, I can't persuade her. I tell her the solemn truth, as I tell you . . . the only happy Brits today are ex-pat Brits . . . I mean at your and my level. Not chairmen of gas or water . . . Ex-pats. [What d'you do?

Prince Unemployed . . .

Greg You see! What's your line?

Prince Jus' left school, ain't I?

Greg Look. Quit. Cross the Channel and backpack down to Malaga.

He hands him a card.]

Buzz my buzzer and I guarantee you'll have a week's bed and meals till you're on your feet. You'll love it. We laugh a lot. They say money doesn't bring happiness . . . they're lying. We jump in the Med and we laugh and laugh . . . we laugh through the food and the wine and the sex . . . and the sun is always there! Right?

The Dogs by Donal O'Kelly

Turkey, any age, any accent.

This is a rather abstract play – a family gathering for the
'Christmas lunch from hell' – where the turkey, the rat and
the deceased dogs can talk.

The Macken family are falling apart and everything is
compounded by the tension around the Christmas lunch.
The family are trying to carry out the turkey-eating
imperative, representing holding it all together, and the two
ghostly dogs are trying to prevent its consumption.

Turkey is imperious, scathing, disgusted by the humans
and their seasonal appalling behaviour, and certainly calls
the shots in the animal-speaking kingdom, even though he
is trussed and ready for the oven.

This is an Irish family, but you could easily transfer the
colloquialism to fit your own accent – for example, 'ye heat
yere fours' to 'you heat your fires'.

'Trystfist' is a play on words around 'Christmas', which is
actually, according to the turkey, all about fighting,
drinking and sentimentality.

Turkey   Naked, limp and plump I lie, vacuum-plucked – indignity! Still frozen from my fridge-time, but warming to my coming feastery, surrounded on the good butcher's fleck formica by my turkey-brethren – my disciples, my prophets, my leaders, my followers, my fellows, my rivals, my one-in-all, my all-in-one, my partners in the Trystfist.

I spread myself among the ovens of the Trystian world. My feet are bound. My hole is stuffed. Potatoes in tinfoil surround me.

Every year ye welcome me, yet heat yere fours.

Every year ye prepare and embellish me, ripe for the feast.

Ye have flamed me, ye have taken nourishment and pleasure from my hot flesh, year after year ye have enjoyed my meat.

I do not mind. I feel no pain. My sacrifice is done according to my will.

Eat of my breast! Wrench my legs asunder! Sink yere teeth and dentures into my thighs ye are wont to call my drumsticks! Devour my burnt remains! Leave only the bones, the bones, the bygones, until the next year, again the ovens, again the consume, again the throw out the bones, sowing the seeds for the do it again the next year again from the flames we arise, phoenix-lick, the eternal regeneration of the Trystkiss bird, each year triumphant again for ever and ever.

Dogs Barking by Richard Zajdlic

Ray, early thirties, any accent.

Ray is Neil's mate. Like dogs that bark to appear fierce, Neil is engaged in a war of attrition with his ex-girlfriend Alex, which seems to be about ownership of property, but is more about ownership of Alex. Neil is trying to claim the flat he used to share with his mortgage-paying ex by moving himself in and her possessions out while she is absent. To do this he recruits his frequently exploited van-owning friend Ray. Naive and kind-hearted, Ray has himself been ousted from his marital home by his wife's new boyfriend and is now being pursued by the Child Support Agency. With a large frame running rapidly to fat and sexual frustration borne out of his estrangement, he comforts himself with beer and carbohydrates, hence a painful knee condition and a tendency to whinge.

Here he's talking to Alex. He's hanging around her flat aware of her new and sudden availability. Ray responds to Alex's polite interest in his problems, unaware she's trying to get him to leave. A more genuine character than Neil, Ray really does feel the pain he describes, and in his account of both his isolation from his children and his legal requirement to pay crippling amounts towards their comfortable life with another man while he goes without, he comes close to tears.

It's important here to draw Ray's distress from his wonderment at how this could have happened to him, rather than self-pity for his predicament. Although there is a wryness there, he should be a mainly sympathetic, if woeful, character.

Ray Gail put the CSA on me, didn't she? (*Scoffs.*) Fucking insult, innit? I buy everything for them kids – all the extras – on top of what I give her anyway.

[**Alan** Yes?]

Ray Yeah. New shoes, coats – there ain't a weekend when one of them's not saying, 'Mummy said you had to buy us this.' I mean, fair enough, they're my kids only now I got this bunch of arseholes telling me I got to give her even more 'cos she's struggling to make ends meet. It's just bollocks, innit? Kids are in school now, she's working again, and living with this other bloke – and he's doing alright – better than me. I mean, she ain't struggling that much if every half-term she packs the kids off to me and fucks off abroad with matey boy. I ain't had a holiday in five years – she's been to Greece, Corfu, Thailand, they even went to American once. Just them, mind, not the kids.

[**Alex** No?]

Ray No. Tell a lie. She took 'em to Spain once. They liked that. Showed me the photos and everything. Nice, that was. My wife. My kids. And him. It's not right, is it? (*Beat.*) I never hit her. Or cheated on her. I just . . . bored her. Why the fuck am I paying for that?

He realises with horror he might cry. He moves away, embarrassed. **Alex** *has stopped her work, sympathetic now.*

Fucking hell. Went off on one there. Sorry.

Five Kinds of Silence by Shelagh Stephenson

Billy, forty to sixty, any accent.

This is a play about retribution and rebirth – the killing of an abusive father, Billy, by his two daughters and the rebuilding of their and their mother's lives. It is a complex and surprising insight into the damaged abuser as well as the damaged abused; Billy's commentary to the audience forms a monologue weaving in and out of the drama, his story told from his own unique perspective.

Billy is relating his younger years in what was a smothering, corrupting and literally dreadful youth. The description of his life as a child is offered to the listener in an intimate and brutally remorseless way, and the lack of compassion or kindness in his telling go some way to explaining the monster that is Billy the adult. There is delicious opportunity in this piece to inhabit every character in the description without losing the momentum of this as a narrative.

It is important to know that Billy is already dead, the daughters shoot him in the opening scene of the play. He tells his story with a dispassionate hindsight as he remembers witnessing a séance as a child and the punishment meted out to him for being disobedient.

Billy I don't remember pain, I don't remember pleasure. I was born aged six with teeth and a black, black heart. I'm what, eight? She has a new man now, a soft milky thing, no match for my lost blind dad. He winds wool for her with his limp fish hands. A voice like gruel. Boneless he is. And yet. And yet – Dark . . . feet like blocks of ice, heart bumping against my throat. Voices burbling in the blackness, Is anybody there? Is anybody there? They got a drowned man once, he spoke with weeds tangled in his throat, I heard him. He opens his mouth and it's not his voice come out it's dead people. Not frightened, me, I'm just cold, that's what that banging noise is in my chest. Dry tongue. Stupid bastards don't know I'm here. Stupid bastards. There's someone coming through, he says, there's someone coming through, it's a man. Stupid bastards, I don't believe them, I wish someone would put the light on the skin's going tight on the top of my head I think I'm having a heart attack, MAM! Billy? Is that you? Let me stay, I want to stay, I won't make no noise. I told you, bloody bugger, I told you. She's pulling me, dragging me upstairs, I'm fighting back, bloody get off me, bloody get off. No don't shut me up in the dark, it's black in there, the black gets in my nose and mouth and eyes, I can't breathe. She says get in the cupboard, you'll have no light, you don't deserve it. Bloody bugger bastard, I shout, bloody damn bugger. Crack. She hits me. Crack. Keep your fury, Billy, she says, you'll need it out there, but never cry, or I'll send the devil to you. No, no, I won't cry, don't send him, I don't want to see him, don't shut the door, what if he comes, Mam, what if he comes? But she slams the door anyway. I won't cry, I shout, I bloody won't. Bastards . . . bloody damn blast shit bastards . . . don't send the devil to me, I don't want to see him . . . bloody bugger pig devil, I bloody am not I bloody am not I bloody am not frightened you buggers – you pig buggers.

Flush by David Dipper

Francis, late teens to early twenties, London accent.

Flush dramatises the sexually predatory world inhabited by three poker-playing friends in contemporary London. Poker is a game of bluffs and gambles, victories and losses, much like their lives.

Francis is deeply troubled. He has raped and left for dead Lily, the sister of his friend Charlie. Francis's accomplice was his gay lover, Cupid. Their relationship is a secret, as these two are members of a clique of hard-playing, fiercely heterosexual young men who meet once a week to play poker. Lily had discovered them in a compromising situation: had she told anyone, and she was likely to, they would have been finished. Francis never liked her, but he has had no peace since her death. To compound his torment, he suspects the girlfriend he loves, Holly, of having a relationship with Cupid – Cupid would do this as a way of wielding power. He is also a much better poker player than Francis; everyone is.

This monologue comes at the peak of Francis' distress as he tries to come to terms with the unbearable guilt he is carrying over Lily's death.

Francis So she's lying on my chest in bed, 'cause Holly loves falling asleep on me, and I'm cuddling her and out of nowhere she tells me about her first time. 'Cause she was only sixteen at this party and she was drunk. And this bloke and his mate decide to take advantage. And she tells me about it and I listen to her.

I listen to everything.

And I think about it and I imagine it. And I want to cry.

And after a while she falls asleep.

And I begin to sob my heart and I hold her and kiss her and cry like I've never. Or will ever. And she wakes up and asks me what's the matter. But all I can do is cry.

So I write a confession and address it to Charlie, but that doesn't do it justice. So I go out and I lose a hundred and twenty quid. But that doesn't do it justice. So the next night I go out and lose a hundred and fifty quid, but that doesn't do it justice. So the next night I go out and hit some ex-public-school boy and when he doesn't get up I hit his friend and when he doesn't get up I start on someone else, but that doesn't do it justice and I start to realise what this is I've got to carry around. And I start to realise how fucking long my life is and I walk straight to the top of a multi-storey and I honest to God think about jumping off. But that doesn't do it justice, so I jump.

And when I hit the ground I die.

And I lay back and think thank fuck for that.

And everything is quiet.

Beautifully quiet.

And everyone wishes they'd died sooner.

And I float.

And I kiss my mother and she is crying, and I kiss my dad and my sister and they are crying and they wave me goodbye and I float.

Frozen by Briony Lavery

Ralph, forties, any accent.

This is a play that investigates the criminal mind and puts three people directly connected – Ralph, Nancy and Agnetha – under the microscope as they interact. Nancy is the mother of a child abused and then murdered by Ralph, and Agnetha is an American psychologist who is developing and lecturing on a theory of criminal insanity. Her thesis is entitled 'Serial Killing: A Forgivable Act'.

Here – the first time we meet Ralph in the play – he is reliving the exact feelings he experiences on seeing a potential young victim. Although it is written in a poetic form, this is just how he speaks, it is very 'real', and one should resist playing the sinister strain throughout. Ralph is an unremarkable man in many respects, a bit of a loner, a big fan of tattoos, but not an obvious killer. The very ordinariness is what makes the speech so chilling. He is in his room, washing his hands at a sink and talking to himself.

Ralph

I just see her
and decide
I'm going to get her in the van.
I just want to keep her for a bit
spend some time with her.
I just do it.
It's a rush of blood.
Hello.

I said 'Hello'
are you deaf?
It's rude to ignore people.
Are you loony?
You're loony.
I'm only being polite.
No need to get the hump.
Not with me.
I just said 'Hello.'
Hello.
Hello.
Hello.
I'm saying 'hello' to you.
Least you can do is make conversation.
Kind of world is this
folk can't be sociable?
Polite.
Least you can do is make a response.
It's Bad Manners if you don't.
Bad manners.
Rude.
I said 'Hello.'
Hello.
Hello.
Hello.
Hello.

Hello then . . .
finally . . .
finally . . .
she goes
'Hello.'

I think she quite liked me.

Oh yes
she was interested.

The van's down here
obviously
the back door's not locked
because I've thought ahead
obviously
she wants to come
it's only fifty yards
it's convenient.

I've got cushions in the back
And a sleeping bag.
Obviously.

Sometimes you're fucked by
circumstances
things don't go your way.

Picks something up. Regards it.

The secateurs
I don't bargain for
but
in the event
they turn out
useful
and add to it all
passing off
efficiently

but
logistically
she's persuaded it's time
to get in the van
you make it work
she's in the van.

A sound of deliberate snipping of plants . . .
He puts the top on the bottle of hand lotion.
Secures it.

Lovely evening.
Sunny . . . but with a light southerly breeze . . .

Germinal by Émile Zola (adapted by William Gaminara)

Souvarine, thirties/forties, an Eastern European accent would be best.

This classic French novel tells the story of a coal-mining community in northern France in 1866/7 and of the colliers' fight in miserable conditions against the mine owners primarily, but also the middle classes – managers and shopkeepers – who exploit them.

Souvarine works and lives among the oppressed French workers, having left his native Russia out of necessity. A true anarchist and committed revolutionary, he lives for the day the world order changes and the working man will break free of his chains. He will stop at nothing to achieve this, but bides his time for the right moment. Despite everything Souvarine is a sensitive and kind man, traumatised by lost love, which only hardens his resolve. Here he is talking to Etienne, the migrant worker who for a time seemed to be shaking things up at the pit – he initiated a strike which was eventually broken by military force. Souvarine hopes Etienne will stay strong but fears he'll go back to work for the sake of their co-worker Catherine, with whom he is in love. Souvarine tells this story as a parable, shortly before he leaves for good. Focusing on the intention here will prevent the performance becoming too sentimental and tragic.

Souvarine You see our plans went wrong. We spent fourteen days hiding in a hole in the ground, tearing the soil from beneath the railway line; but we were given bad information, and instead of the Imperial train it was an ordinary passenger train that blew up; eighty-seven people were killed. Annushka used to bring us food in the hole, she even lit the fuse because we did not think they would suspect a woman. They arrested her six days later. Every day after that, I followed the trail, hidden amongst the crowd listening to every word that was spoken. Twice I almost shouted out and leaped over their heads to join her. But it would have been no use. One man less is one soldier less and I could tell that each time her eyes met mine she was saying no. On her last day, in the public place, I was also there right at the back; she was the fifth in turn. Only because it was raining the rope kept breaking over and over again; they took twenty minutes to hang the first four. She could not see me at first so I stood on a large stone and stared at her until she caught sight of me. And from that moment on our eyes never left each other, even after the floor was removed from beneath her feet and her body was left dangling in mid-air, her eyes continued to stare into mine. And it wasn't until the wind turned her head to one side that I was able to wave my hat and walk away. That was her punishment for lighting the fuse, and our punishment for loving each other too much. Now I know her death was a good thing, her blood will inspire heroes and heroines in years to come; and for me . . . I have no weaknesses left in my heart, nothing at all . . . no family, no wife, nothing that will make my hands shake on the day when they most need to be steady.

Girl, Watching by Jyll Bradley

Wight, sixty. 'He is middle class, from a family where there was once money. So he has the accent still, but not the resources' (author's note).

The watching girl of the title is fourteen-year-old Anna, who has observed secretly, while birdwatching, her mother's oldest friend, Sibylla. The narrative of the play surrounds this woman, who has run away to a remote coastal summer house after learning of her husband David's unfaithfulness. Her dramatic departure brings old secrets and resentments to the surface for Anna's parents, Wight and Polly, forcing them both to accept painful truths that will divide them for ever: it's not just Anna who has been watching.

In the preceding part of this long speech, Wight has told Polly that he's always hated David, despite their long-apparent friendship since meeting as soldiers during the war. Now he explains how he's known for years that she and David were lovers and that David is the real father of Anna. He explains that he discovered her affair by chance, but has put up with Polly's faithlessness, knowing he could never match up to David and not wanting to lose her completely by bringing the truth out into the open. However, since Sibylla's flight, David has finally left the area, asking Wight to say goodbye to Polly for him and tacitly acknowledging that he knows Wight is aware of his betrayal. Wight knows the affair is over and that he can finally speak. Accordingly, years of suppressed feelings emerge with calm acceptance and no little dignity.

It is clear that the visual images of the day Wight describes are burnt indelibly into his memory.

Wight I saw the two of you together once at Silversands. I drove out there one day, I don't know why. I'd been valuing some farmland up on the Downs, and I'd finished early. Driving off and instead of cutting onto the new bit of motorway, towards home, I found myself on the old coast road. Before I knew it I was driving off the ferry, onto the island. It was a perfect summer's afternoon. Up by the windmill and on through the marshes. I parked at the foot of the track, walked the last half-mile, across the beach, up into the dunes. (*Beat.*) You can get a good view of the house from the dunes. And you can't be seen. (*Beat.*) The sun lounge door was open. There were some muslin curtains hanging and there was a gentle breeze and they lifted and they parted and there you were with him. I stood, watching you . . . (*Beat.*) Then I turned and walked away. Climbed away. That soft climbing way you walk in dunes. There were some little wading birds – unusual – plovers? nesting on the beach. Small and dainty like tiny painted toys, they were – running in and out of the tide. I've often wondered if they return. (*Beat.*) I should have walked out to the cottage then and there. Confronted David. Driven you home.

Pause.

(*Laughing.*) . . . if I turned a blind eye things would run their course . . .

Pause.

You came home late, (*Laughing.*) you'd been so busy at the shop with Sibylla . . . (*Beat.*) She really didn't know until the blow-up last summer. In her own little whimsical, irritating world. Actually, I rather liked her. She was always perfectly pleasant to me. (*Laughing.*) Could never remember my name.

Kiss Me Like You Mean It by Chris Chibnall

Tony, twenty-five, Manchester accent.

The underlying theme of this play is *carpe diem*, and much of it takes place in the garden of a large terraced house during a party. Tony has just met Ruth at the party. He has come along not expecting any major change to his life, one that's infinitely precious now that the testicular cancer that threatened it is in remission. It's the early hours of a summer morning and they're alone in the open air. She's very attractive and he's smitten. He's tried to impress her but has only succeeded in showing himself up, nearly setting light to her with his unpredictable Zippo lighter and his lack of cool.

They seem to be getting on quite well, despite the fact that Ruth's boyfriend is inside the house, until Tony admits his girlfriend is there too and this late piece of news drives Ruth indoors in a huff.

Tony gets talking to Don, an elderly man from an upstairs flat, who remonstrates with him for his lack of initiative. Unbeknown to Tony, Don and his wife Edie are planning a suicide pact at dawn: Don is dying and Edie doesn't want to live without him, and Don tries to impress on Tony the need to take nothing for granted. Reminded of the need to grasp life when the opportunity presents itself, Tony, a hopeless romantic, decides to confess his love to this woman who has completely bowled him over, before the fleeting moment passes. In this speech, he declares himself passionately and with conviction, knowing how preposterous his offer may seem, but trusting in his own sincerity, not knowing to the very end whether she'll take the bait.

Tony Listen . . . I need to . . . um . . . say . . . I mean . . . I know we only met earlier . . . And I nearly set you on fire . . . And we're both going out with people. Obviously that's quite tricky. But . . . Well . . . You are the most beautiful woman I have ever laid eyes on in my entire life. I saw you and my heart leapt. You make me want to change my life. To . . . participate. I know it's not possible and that you have a boyfriend and we're not . . . compatible or whatever but . . . I just . . . I know it's stupid . . . but maybe just hear me out for a second and then you can tell me I'm an idiot and we'll both go back in and pretend this never happened but . . . I want to travel the world with you. I want to bring the ice-cold Amstel to your Greek shore. And sit in silence and sip with you. I want to go to Tesco's with you of a Sunday. Watch you sleep, scrub your back, rub your shoulders, suck your toes. I want to write crap poetry about you, lay my coat over puddles for you, always have a handkerchief available for you. I want to get drunk and bore my friends about you, I want them to phone up and moan about how little they see me because I'm spending so much time with you. I want to feel the tingle of our lips meeting, the lock of our eyes joining, the fizz of our fingertips touching. I want to touch your fat tummy and tell you you look gorgeous in maternity dresses, I want to stand next to you wide-eyed and hold my nose as we open that first used nappy, I want to watch you grow old and love you more and more each day. I want to fall in love with you. I think I could. And I think it would be good. And I want you to say yes. You might feel the same.

Beat.

Could you? Maybe?

The Lieutenant of Inishmore by Martin McDonagh

Padraic, twenty-one, Galway accent.

In this darkly comic and often shockingly violent play, we meet 'mad' chip-shop bomber Padraic, the eponymous and self-styled Lieutenant, who has formed his own single-handed splinter group from the Irish National Liberation Army, in his personal quest to hunt down and punish drug takers, peddlers and pushers. The play pivots around the mysterious death of his cat, Wee Thomas, and attempts by others to hide both the fact and, later, the identity of the perpetrator.

In this scene we see him at his most crusading and vengeful, removing the toenails from the upside-down James as a penalty for selling drugs to schoolchildren. Much of the humour comes from the juxtaposition of Padraic's sadistic calling and his commitment to politeness, fairness and consideration. Here he goes into detail describing the execution of his task, but at the same time giving helpful medical advice.

As the author says, Padraic loves his cat more than life itself and that should be kept in mind when approaching this slightly surreal character. It must also be remembered that he shoots in the head both men whom he thinks are responsible for the cat's death, and one of them is his father.

Padraic James Hanley, don't keep going on about your stupid fecking toenails! The way you talk it sounds as if I took off a rake of them, when it was only two I took off, and them only small ones. If they'd been big ones I could understand, but they weren't. They were small. You'd hardly notice them gone. And if it was so concerned you were about the health of them toenails it would've been once in a while you cleaned out the muck from under them.

[**James** Well, you've saved me that job for good now anyways.]

Padraic If I hadn't been such a nice fella I would've taken one toenail off of separate feet, but I didn't, I took two toenails off the one foot, so that it's only the one foot you'll have to be limping on and not the two. If it had been the two you'd've found it a devil to be getting about. But with the pain concentrated on the one, if you can get hold of a crutch or a decent stick, I'm not sure if the General Hospital does hand them out but they might do, I don't know. You could phone them up and ask, or go in and see them would be the best thing, and make sure them toes won't be going septic at the same time. I didn't disinfect this razor at all, I never do, I see no need, but they'd be the best people to ask, sure they're the experts. You'll probably need a tetanus job too, oh there's no question. I do hate injections, I do. I think I'd rather be slashed with a razor than have an injection. I don't know why. Of course, I'd rather have neither. You'll have had both by the end of the day. What a bad day you've had. (*Pause.*) But, em . . . I have lost me train of thought now, so I have.

Little Sweet Thing by Roy Williams

Jamal, late teens, London accent.

This play investigates what it is to survive the inner-London gang culture that surrounds and informs young people today.

Jamal is the local bad boy, a mixed race would-be gangster. He left school early, has little respect for anything or anyone, and makes a decent living as the local drugs dealer. The latest mobile phones, a smart car, good clothes and cash in his pocket: he is a winner. He wields a tremendous power locally, is ruthless with anyone who crosses him and still loves Angela, the woman he is describing in this monologue. She is so different to everyone else, and he even respects her wishes to leave her alone now they have split up. He is talking to his old friend Kev, who has recently come out of prison and has turned over a new leaf, much to Jamal's disgust, stacking shelves in the local shop and planning to go back to school to take some qualifications. Kev has recently started dating Angela. Jamal is checking out his intentions.

Jamal   There's this girl I was seein. She was nice. Had a brain man, so big, smart, knows shit. Anyhow, I knew she weren't the type that would let you rush it, but you know, the more she won't, the more you want to. I took her out one night, to this banging restaurant, make her feel sweet, me as well. I was nervous. Gal made me nervous, I shoulda known summin was up with even then. Anyhow, we're inside yeah, and there's this mile-long queue of people in front, all getting vex cos the restaurant has somehow messed up their group bookings. There was this young waitress girl at the front dealing with it all, dizzy sort, making things worse. Couldn't speak much English either. I was well up for hitting somebody and it was gonna be this waitress. First time ever, I made an effort to take a girl out, and she's screwing it up. Anyhow, this girl, my date, it's like she could read minds, Kev, she strokes the side of my face, like she's saying, 'Nuttin's gonna spoil tonight, nuttin can, calm yerself down.' And I did. Like her words put me in a trance. Next thing I know, she makes her way to the front of the people, starts helping this girl sort the orders out, speaking in French to her. Then she's laughing and chatting with the rest of the other people, calming them down, all I could was watch her, Kev. Thinking to myself, how did she do that, how . . . I couldn't, if it was juss me deh, I'd be cussing and fighting my way out of there by then. Not her. Not many black chicks I know could do that, you nuh, Kev, only the ones who got summin going on inside there. She had it, whatever it is. A gift. I knew, right there and then how loved up I was. When things got mad, and they always do, I could always go to her, escape fer a bit. Cuddle up. You know, feel normal.

[**Kev**   I didn't know she was your woman.]

Jamal   You'll find out, Angela ain't nobody's woman. But there were some things she wanted I just couldn't give, you understand? So according to her, I don't have much of a say in who steps to her from now on, if any, right? I know that. But I need to ask you summin, yeah, and I need you to ask me honestly. You like her?

Lovers and Other Strangers by Renée Taylor and Joseph Bologna

Mike (He), late twenties, American, but any accent (with slight adjustments) would work.

This speech comes from a play that is a compilation of short scenes that investigate some very different relationships between lovers.

Mike is described as big, energetic, masculine, open and sensitive. It is four days before his wedding to Susan – whom he does love in spite of this tirade. It is four o'clock in the morning when he calls round unexpectedly; his insecurity is such that he half expects her to be with another man.

By the end of the scene, they are a solid couple again as they resume discussion around wedding plans – it is as if the outburst had never happened.

He Please don't make me marry you! I know this wedding is costing your parents a lot of money, but I'll pay back every penny of it . . . Look I've got about twenty dollars on me. Here, take it as a deposit . . . and take my watch . . . and I want you to keep the ring. I know when a fella breaks up with a girl, he's supposed to get the ring back, but you can have the ring. That's fair, isn't it? I mean, another guy wouldn't do that, would he, Susan?

Please stop looking at me like that. You shouldn't take it personally. It's nothing against you. It's the times we live in. India's overpopulated! We'll all be sterilized soon. The suicide rate is up. The air is polluted. Is that the kind of world you want to get married in? Is it, Susan? Is it? . . . I know what you're trying to do – make me look like the bad one. Well, it won't work. It won't work. Because I'm clean. I'm clean. You knew exactly what you were doing. You knew I was a confirmed bachelor. You knew I had trouble getting involved, but that didn't stop you. No, not you, baby. You decided to marry me and that was it. Well, who do you think you are, playing God with another person's life? Well, I have no pity for you. None whatsoever, because you're getting just what you deserve. So, get off my back. I owe you nothing, baby. Get it? I owe you nothing!

Give me a break. Take the pressure off me. Call the wedding off. Everything was going along great. We were having fun and smelling flowers. We could go on having fun for years . . . And then some day maybe I'll have a lot of drinks and we could just sneak down to City Hall. That way I won't feel like I'm married. What do you say, Susan? Huh, Suan? What do you say?

All right, Susan. I've got to put my cards on the table. I didn't want to tell you this because I didn't want to hurt your feelings. You're just not dream girl. I'm sorry. I wish you were, but let's face it, Susan. My heart doesn't beat when you come into a room. I don't get goose pimples when I touch you. I'm just not nervous when I'm with you. You're too vulnerable. You're too human. You've got too many problems. And, Susan, there's something about you that really bothers me. Maybe it wouldn't be important to another guy, but I think about it a lot. Susan, you have very thin arms.

So, I don't think I could be faithful. I mean, I want to be faithful, but I just don't think I can. Ever since we got engaged, I walk down the street and I want to grab every ass I see. That's not normal. If you were my dream girl, I'd never give other women a second thought. Don't you understand, I need somebody more perfect, then it wouldn't be so much work for me to love and be faithful. I could just show up.

Look, you'll get over me. After a while, you'll find another boy. Just promise me you won't sleep with anyone until you get married. Will you promise me that, Susan? Will you?

That's it. It's all over. (*He picks up her hand and shakes it.*) Goodbye. I'm sorry. That's it.

Man with Travel Hairdryer by Katie Hims

Dean, thirty-two, any accent.

Hims's play for radio centres around Dean, a police officer who has shot and killed a man in the line of duty, and the reactions of the family and fiancée of the dead man.

His victim, Bodie, appeared to be carrying a gun and was a suspect in an earlier incident. Called out as a member of an armed response team, Dean took the initiative in good faith, followed procedure and opened fire. Later it's discovered that the 'gun' was really a travel hairdryer in a carrier bag, which Bodie was collecting from the mender's.

Months later Dean awaits the decision of a tribunal to determine whether he acted legally. Although he knows he acted professionally he is consumed by a guilt that he can't articulate. There are blanks in his memory and the knowledge that something went wrong contributes to his obsessive thoughts and resulting sexual impotency.

At this point in the drama we hear Dean's thoughts inside his head. He marvels at his own strength and his conviction that he would do the same thing again if necessary, but he's deluding himself and later he confesses he cannot kill even a fly. Although he talks of coping, it is apparent – not least to his wife – that he is heading for a breakdown. Now with a permanently shaven head, out of empathy for Bodie's fiancée's shock-induced complete hair loss, he's clearly unaware of the threatening and unsympathetic picture he presents. Both the content and the manner of the speech are indicative of his growing mental instability.

This is a valuable opportunity for performing close, intimate work at the microphone.

Dean I used to ask myself. Before. I used to ask myself could I ever shoot anyone and now I know the answer but could I shoot someone again? And the answer again is I don't know. And it's surprising really. I mean the whole thing is surprising. I think I've surprised a lot of people. You know in the way that I've reacted. Because I would never have predicted I'd be like this. That it would be this strong. Because I wasn't like that. I was never like that before. And during the exam. The firearms exam. A lot of them needed talcum powder. For their hands. Like a gymnast on the asymmetric bars. So that the gun didn't slip. But not me. Cos I just didn't get ruffled. And they used to call me Sure. Honestly they did. I'm not making this up. And the people who didn't know used to say is that your surname then? Is it Dean Shaw? And I'd say no, it's Dean Stokoe. And they'd say so why they calling you Shaw? Then I'd tell them. I'd tell them why. It's cos of the deodorant. They used to laugh. People used to think nothing winds him up. Nothing gets to him . . . My wife says to me what are you going to wear to the inquest and I say I think I'll wear my suit. And she looks sort of relieved when I say this. Like she thought I might be planning to go dressed as Elvis. That's good says my wife. You look good in your suit. And she smiles at me. She smiles nervously. Sometimes I think she is a bit afraid of me.

Modern Dance for Beginners by Sarah Phelps

Russell, thirty-six, any accent.

This intriguing play depends on the convention of using two actors to play all the characters in a succession of related scenes which tell a story that comes full circle. The particular plot here centres on a group of twenty-first-century young, vibrant, rather selfish, urban professionals, who take what they want from life with little regard for the consequences.

Russell is described as 'a faithful media executive and terminal romantic'. He and Frances work in the same office and have been having a relationship based solely on mutual sexual gratification for some months. Intense pressure from his boss and a sense of inevitability that he'll lose his job has finally got to Russell. He's lost his libido, but ironically not his ability to perform. Suddenly all the shallow pleasures of his life disinterest him and he longs to make an emotional connection with Frances. She, however, is only interested in maintaining the sexual status quo; she is secretly still in love with her ex, Owen, who has recently married someone else.

Here, the couple are in bed, having interrupted their lovemaking due to Russell's lack of concentration. He wants to talk; he knows Frances doesn't reciprocate his feelings, but in this speech he appeals to her to understand his commitment, which transcends raw sex and yearns for the togetherness that she despises. Revealing his obsession for watching her closely in public and private, he expresses his need to do normal couple things openly, to stop other men invading his territory and to bring their relationship to another level.

Russell I walk past you in corridors and you don't even flicker, not even a sideways glance and I know you.

[**Frances** You don't.]

Russell I know how your skin flushes. I know you've got a birthmark on the back of your thigh that looks like Pete Postlethwaite in profile. Counts for something. We sit at work and no one knows. About us. And what we have. Everyone's going on about who's going to be out the door and did he jump or was he pushed and all I can think about is that some days your breasts . . . tits get swollen. The nipples are tender. You wince. There's a faint blue vein that runs across, it gets more pronounced. Closer to the surface of the skin. I think about that at work. It drives me crazy. I don't do a bloody stroke all day. If that bastard Skinner knew just how little I do, he'd throttle me. I deserve to get the sack. All I think about is that little blue vein and the pulse underneath it. But I'm more gentle then. Do you notice? Are you aware that I notice?

[**Frances** No.]

Russell I just think it's a waste. To know each other this well, to be this intimate and not . . . develop it –

[**Frances** Russ, this isn't intimacy. It's forensic science!

Russell Alright but it's a start, isn't it?

Beat.

Frances A start to what?]

Russell You and me. I want to do girlfriend-boyfriend stuff. You know. Go out in public. I'd like that. Go to the pictures. Go on the London Eye and snog all the way round. Have a dirty weekend in Blackpool and go on a roller coaster. Go up the river on a boat. Stay over at night. Talk to you in the bath. Tell stupid jokes. Rub your back when you get period pains. Watch you sleep. What the fuck, whatever.

No End of Blame by Howard Baker

Grigor, eighteen, any accent.

This is the opening speech of a play that explores the artist's moral responsibility in society.

It is 1918, a remote place in the Carpathian Mountains. The dishevelled, war-worn Grigor and his comrade and dear friend Bela (pronounced Beela) are soldiers in the Hungarian Infantry. Battle is still going on in the distance but they have managed to escape the worst of it. Both passionate about art, Grigor is sketching as if his life depended on it. Though the subject is normally a fellow soldier, he has captured a local woman and forced her to strip for some life-drawing practice. He wants his friend to get as much out of it as he is doing, though for Grigor it is strictly the form of the woman's body that he is enjoying, an artist's appreciation, not the appreciation of a man who hasn't seen a naked woman for years. Grigor threatens her with the rifle and does a good job of petrifying her, but he is in fact highly moralistic, peace-loving and has managed to get through the entire war without taking a single life.

Grigor (*shouts*)   Come on! Where are you! Just look at her! Just look at her breasts! I love her breasts, they go – they're like – they're utterly – harmonious – they fall – they sag – not sag – sink – not sag or sink – they – *Concede* – that's what they do – *Concede* – they are completely harmonious with gravity – *Where Are You*? They are in total sympathy with –

[*The* **Woman** *grabs her clothes and tries to run away.* **Grigor** *leaps to his feet and grabs his rifle.*]

Don't run away!

[*She freezes. he drops the rifle, goes back to sketching.*]

She keeps trying to run away – I wish I spoke Roumanian, is it – I'd say, look I'm an artist, I don't kill girls – not that she's a girl, she's a woman, thank God – I can't draw girls – I hate girls – there's no concession in their flesh – too much defiance – everything pokes upwards – nipples, tits, bum – everything goes upwards – all aspiration, ugh –

[*She tries to escape again. He grabs the rifle.*]

Don't run away! (*She freezes*). Sorry – sorry – (*He throws down the rifle, picks up his sketchpad again.*) Look at her buttocks – Bela, look at them – do look at them – see what I say –

[**Bela** *comes in, holding a sketchbook limply in his hand. He also wears a threadbare tunic.*]

the female body accepts – concedes to gravity – is in profoundly intimate relations with the earth – the curve, you see – the curve is the most perfect line – eliminates all tension – *why don't you draw*! No, I haven't got it – haven't got it – no – (*He tears off a sheet, starts another.*) I am so sick of drawing men – soldiers bathing – never again – I have eighteen books of soldiers bathing – eighteen! – in my pack – (*He scuttles to a new position.*) – there, you see – the essential female line – the curve – does not resist but – (**Bela** *moves closer to the woman.*) Bela – (**Bela** *is staring at her.*) Bela – you are in my view – (*He does not move.*) My fucking view!

Osama the Hero by Dennis Kelly

Francis, late twenties, any accent.

Far from being a vindication of al-Qaida, this play is about the climate of fear in our own society; a visceral and urgent exploration of what can happen when an individual dares to see the world differently in a climate of seemingly universal tension.

Francis is interrogating seventeen-year-old Gary, a young man with some problems – he is ostracised at school for being a 'weirdo'. Francis is a vigilante; he operates on a sink estate where he suspects Gary to be guilty of terrorism. Someone is blowing up the garages and putting bombs in the waste bins. As Gary seems to have been saying all the wrong things at school with regard to terrorism and suggesting support for Osama bin Laden, who is, according to Gary, a committed freedom fighter, the finger has been pointed at him.

But Gary is only guilty of seeing everything for how it is and voicing that; he is an innocent. Francis is obsessed with ridding the streets of all terrorists, rapists and perverts. His father died while in prison for attacking a known paedophile. He was a local hard case and hero to his son and in this speech Francis wants to communicate to the bound and gagged Gary that he is continuing the good fight in his father's place.

Francis   D'you know who I am?

No answer.

Oi.

Oi.

Oi, you.

S'alright, I'm just asking you a question.

[**Gary** *looks at him.*]

Francis   D'you know who I am?

[**Gary** *shakes his head.*]

Francis   Seriously, d'you know who I am?

[**Gary** *shakes his head.*]

Francis   Seriously, d'you know who I am? Have you heard of me?

[**Gary** *shakes his head.*]

Francis   Look this isn't –

I'm not gonna –

I'm just asking if you've heard of me, that's all.

[**Gary** *shakes his head.*]

Francis   Don't shake your head coz that's just winding me up.

[**Gary** *doesn't know what to do.*]

Francis   I'm just asking if you've heard of me.

Now, don't give me the answer you think I want, because the answer you think I want is not the answer I want. Okay? It's not a test, I'm not gonna hurt you, it's not loaded, I'm just asking you a simple question d'you know who I am.

Do you know who I am?

[**Gary** *doesn't know what to do. Eventually he shakes his head.*]

Francis What you mean, you don't know who I am? How do you not know who I am? So you've got no idea?

[**Gary** *shakes his –*]

Francis Don't shake your head.

So you've got no idea who I am?

Beat.

No one ever said anything to you about me?

Beat.

I know who you are, a piece of shit like you, I know all about you and your little presentation, yes, that's right, we know all about that. We have ears, Gary. And you're saying you haven't even got a fucking clue who I am, like no one on this estate has ever said a word to you about me, ever?

[*Pause.* **Gary** *nods.*]

Francis So no one on this estate ever talks about me, no one ever –

Beat.

You see what happens when you give the answers to questions that you think people want? You get it wrong. You get it wrong, Gary. Honesty is always the best policy.

Pause.

D'you know who my dad was?

[*Pause.* **Gary** *nods.*]

Francis Whose dad, Gary? Whose fucking dad?

No answer

I'm gonna tell you a story about my dad. This one time I brought home a dog, scruffy little mongrel, half staf, my dad never trusted stafs, I'm about eight, never trusted stafs, found him up the field, brought him home and my dad says – that's a staf: that's a staf, that'll turn – but I begged and begged to keep that dog and he says – alright – because he loved me, Gary – alright, you can keep that dog but if anything happens – and he didn't finish his sentence, just if anything happens and that's it. Week later that dog tears into my sister, tears into her, you can still see the scar, you ask her, in here on her upper arm, you ask her, blood . . . blood . . . takes her up the hospital, carries her up the hospital, and I'm at home, hours going by, fucking shitting, dog as well, both shitting it. He comes home, says nothing. Gets the dog, gets me, gets a knife. Goes upstairs. In the the bathroom. Dog in the bath, shaking. Takes my hand, puts it on the dog's jugular, says – feel that pulse? – puts the knife into my other hand. Blood hit the fucking ceiling. Took me forty-five minutes to cut the head off. Another hour to cut the legs off, through the bone. Put it in a bin bag, took it up the field, chucked it in the lake. My dad loved me. He loved my sister. D'you understand that? Gary? Do you understand?

Our Bad Magnet by Douglas Maxwell

Alan, twenty-nine, Scottish accent.

Our Bad Magnet is set in Girvan, a quiet Scottish seaside town, now unfashionable. Alan is one of three former school friends meeting on this day to commemorate the mysterious disappearance ten years before of their friend 'Giggles'. During the course of the drama secrets are revealed, and differing perceptions of past events are argued over.

Alan is the only one who never left their home town. Permanently overweight throughout a play that charts the men's lives through the ages of nine, nineteen and twenty-nine, he has nevertheless, up to this point, lived contentedly with wife Tina, who is currently pregnant.

Here, Alan is talking to Paul and Fraser. They both know that the real father of Tina's child is most likely Paul, who's been having a secret affair with Tina for years. It becomes obvious from later dialogue that Alan also has strong suspicions that this is the case.

This speech comes immediately after an awkward moment when the other two fall out bitterly over their selective memories and opinions of what became of their missing friend. Alan starts by announcing that Tina is pregnant, then reveals painfully that she has rejected it and thereby him. He has a quiet dignity, woven through with an unspoken acceptance that the baby is probably not his.

Some sense of the weightiness of this character would add to the picture of a man to be pitied, although seeking pity should not be the aim in itself. It's also important to remember that the impulse for the speech comes from an argument in which insults fly between the two men to whom this is addressed. It may start as a strategy to defuse the atmosphere, but he can't stop himself from openly confessing his bewilderment.

Alan   Did I tell yous that Tina's pregnant?

They look at him but can't find the words to speak.

Came as a bit of a shocker I can tell you. I'd been away at a battle re-enactment thing. I'd been helping out some of the English Civil war mob down in the black country somewhere. Their organisation was an absolute disgrace. Really it was a fiasco. Most folk didn't even know what side they were on and the kit was just bits of cardboard and Halloween costumes. Anyway, I was meant to be away all weekend but I just headed home Saturday night. I got home to find Tina lying on the bed, greeting her face off. Just crying and crying and crying. She wouldn't say what the hell was wrong. My heart was beating man, I tell you, I thought she'd got cancer or something. She eventually told me she was up the duff. Well I said that's good news! We can afford it, we've got room, good job, we're happy and everything. She . . . she said she didn't want my baby. She loves me and everything, she just doesn't want my baby. (*Pause.*) Dr McCulloch says it happens all the time. Chemicals released into the body and everything. It's difficult. I've to give her room. So I'm in the hut most nights building stuff and thinking about things. She'll come around. Hope.

Peepshow by Isabel Wright

Richard, late twenties, any accent.

The play concerns people living in a city tower block, giving the audience an opportunity to spy on the private lives going on behind the walls, hence the title.

There's an element of mystery about the self-satisfied Richard: partner Sharon doesn't always know where he's been, what he's been doing, where the extra money comes from. Sharon for her part is tired of Richard and would like to move on. He is possessive, though, and observant; he sees things and hears things through the walls and wonders if Sharon's seeing neighbour Ben behind his back. He frequently interrogates her in minute detail, disguising his paranoia with frequent insincere endearments; their sex life is irritable, and emotionally unsatisfying for both.

The songlike quality and structure are intentional and should add to the intimacy of this soliloquy, spoken wordlessly while watching Sharon. The play features many moments of sexual activity and there are erotic images to connect with here too.

Richard   You smell different.

You smell the way you used to smell when we first met.

Your hair is different.

I don't know how.

Don't know about hair.

You smile to yourself.

Hum a tune as you wash up.

Never used to.

You've lost weight.

Why would you want to lose weight?

You get every Monday off work.

You don't call me every lunchtime any more.

We negotiate round each other at breakfast.

I ask you what you're thinking

I ask you what you're thinking

You say, I'm tired. That's all, baby, that's all.

You lie different in bed.

Turned away.

You don't curl your arm round my waist.

You don't kiss me awake.

I ask you what you're thinking

I ask you what you're thinking

You say, I'm tired. I'm tired of . . . I'm tired, baby, that's all.

I watch you when you don't know I'm watching you.

Follow you from work.

A glimpse of your life when you're not with me.

You're ordinary.

Extraordinary.

Asking myself.

How do I

Know if I

Know you at all.

Asking

How do I

Know if I

Know you at all.

The Philanthropist by Christopher Hampton

Philip, thirties, RP accent.

This play is set in the near future: a crazed gunman has assassinated the Prime Minister and most of the Cabinet, but the event hardly makes a ripple in the cosy academic life of Philip, an Oxford don and philosophy specialist. Philip is a good-natured fellow, with an optimistic and non-critical view of everything and everyone, hence his admitted inability to teach English literature. Inevitably, people take advantage of him, and during the course of the events in the play he is forced to confront his own naive complacency.

Philip has held an intimate dinner in his college rooms, for which his much younger fiancée Celia did the cooking. One of the guests, the sexually predatory Araminta, has stayed behind and seduced him, without much resistance. It's not that Philip was complicit in his infidelity, more that his innocence means he doesn't read well the signals others use in place of direct communication.

Here, he's been berated by the indignant Celia who has encountered Araminta in Philip's rooms the morning after the night before. They've been discussing his inadequacies, mainly his inability to understand the arcane way in which women's minds work and Celia's frustration with it all. Poor Philip, the harder he tries the more he upsets people. In a moment of heartfelt candour he confesses his most shameful memory of sexual humiliation, in the hope that Celia will understand his genuine lack of interpersonal skills with women and forgive his inadvertent lapse.

Philip I've always been a failure with women.

[**Celia** Oh, please.

Philip But it's true.]

I remember, I remember the first girl I was ever in love with, Carol her name was, and I made the mistake, just as we were about to go to bed together for the first time, of telling her I was a virgin. Oh, well, then, she said, that was that, she wasn't going to be a guinea-pig for anyone. It was that phrase that did it. She became so entranced and horrified by the idea represented by her own quite fortuitous image, that I gave up, there was obviously no hope. Guinea-pig, 'I'm not going to be a guinea-pig', she kept on saying. So there it was. A whole relationship doomed by a random word-association. This is the same thing. You think I'm being sentimental and self-pitying just because I say I'm a failure with women. But I'm not. I'm just telling the simple truth, which is that I've never managed to give a woman satisfaction. I hope to. I hoped to with you. Given a bit of time. But in itself it's just a perfectly neutral fact. Like the fact I was a virgin when I was with Carol. (*He breaks off for a moment.*) She was very cruel. I adored her.

Real Classy Affair by Nick Grosso

Joey, late twenties, London accent.

A funny and also sinister story of power between pals in Finsbury Park, north London, much of this play takes place in a pub, where four young friends talk about nothing in particular. It is what they don't say that is dangerous, and 'power', however petty, is about credentials and fashion, who is 'in' this week and who 'out'.

This speech comes from the opening scene. Joey never has the power within this group; in fact he is very much the group lackey and deemed to be a bit 'slow' by some of the gang who are very much a 'family'. The lads are described as wearing identical suits, slicked-back short hair, and drinking pints with whiskey chasers. The lads have known each other since school, and they look out for each other.

Joey is an alert and spirited young man whose life is one dramatic happening after another. He has been sent to get a chair for an unexpected friend who has just joined them. Whenever he comes back to his friends, from whatever situation, he always has a story to tell about what has just happened, and it is always extraordinary, much like Joey himself.

Joey   here i found one

They look round at **Joey**.

this woman had her handbag on it – i said excuse me love is this
seat taken? – she said not right now no – i said well i'm *talking* about
right now ain't i i'm not talking about bleeding tomorrow! – she
had fear in her eyes – she said i'm waiting for my husband – i said i
don't care if you're waiting for king bloody tutu . . . ! she started
crying poor dear

[**Harry**   she didn't?]

Joey   she did – she thought i was gonna hit her

[**Harry** *looks shocked.*

Harry   what?]

Joey   she thought i was one of these wife-beaters or something – i
said listen lady do i look the sort who dishes it out cos he ain't got a
chair?

[**Harry**   what did she say?]

Joey   she was shaking – she was looking at my fists – i had em
clenched – i didn't even *realise* – i was standing there with my fists
clenched and she was about ninety-two and she had holes in her
shoes and she was waiting for her ol fella – so i bought her a drink –
she was shaking her *tits* off – she thought i was gonna *kill* her – i
told her i ain't a *murderer* woman – she'd watched too many crime
shows – so i got her a gin and tonic – slice of lemon – she looked
chuffed – i said when your hubby comes you get me and i'll get him
a chair – she was well chuffed – she thought i was mother teresa –
she said he likes a pint of guinness – i said i'll get him a *chair* not a
flaming *drink* you cheeky bitch – i tell ya these ol biddies – you gotta
be careful – show em the slightest bit of kindness and they take libs
– *libs* i tell ya – still i don't expect he'll show – not in this weather –
he's probably crawled up in some corner dying of hypothermia

The Revengers' Comedies by Alan Ayckbourn

Anthony Staxton-Billing, thirty-eight, RP accent.

The 'revengers' of the title are two people thrown together by fate, who discover a common interest in reprisal for injuries committed by others. Their lives become entwined as they go in search of vengeance, resulting in all the confusion one would expect of an Ayckbourn comedy.

Anthony Staxton-Billing is married to Imogen, a fact which hasn't deterred him from an affair with the passionate but self-centred Karen Knightly. Tiring of his mistress, he returns to his wife whom Karen describes as 'ageing and bovine'. Twenty-something and spurned, Karen happens to meet Henry Bell, a forty-something redundant executive while both are attempting suicide at the same spot. Although strangers, they compare woes and ultimately agree, at Karen's urging, to exact revenge on each other's nemesis, to avoid suspicion falling on either of them. For her that's Imogen Staxton-Billing, whom Karen claims has lured Anthony back by devious means.

Unfortunately, when, according to plan, Henry eventually meets the lonely and vulnerable Imogen, he falls in love with her. The fact does not go unnoticed by Anthony: despite being a suave ladies' man, this gentleman farmer still considers his wife his property and does not appreciate being made a fool of in his own social environment. He intercepts Henry at a gymkhana and proceeds to warn him off. Henry fights back, citing Anthony's cruel treatment of Karen as proof of his dishonourable behaviour.

This is Anthony's scathing response, in which he puts Henry right on certain matters, shedding a whole new light on Karen's claims and calling into question her sexual self-control and mental stability. He's indignant at having to defend himself to a man he considers to be both ridiculously naive and his social inferior.

Anthony   Karen Knightly and I had – well, you could hardly term it an affair – had a bit of sex together, let's say – for all of a month. Well, quite a lot of sex, really. We tried out all twenty-five of the bedrooms in that house of hers over the course of about a fortnight, starting in the attic and finishing up in the master suite. She insisted we dressed in suitable clothes to suit different locations. I remember our night in the nursery as particularly bizarre. When we'd completed the course, she declared that according to ancient law we were now legally engaged. And that at the next full moon I had to sacrifice my existing wife Imogen and change my name to Alric the Awesome. At which point, I realized she was stark staring mad and I broke off the relationship. She then plagued us both for months. Writing anonymous letters, drawing strange runes on our front door, phoning up claiming to be a midwife delivering my illegitimate child. You name it, she did it. Culminating, finally, in a phone call demanding that I be on Chelsea Bridge at eight thirty sharp or she would throw herself in the Thames.

[**Henry** (*suspecting a ring of truth in all this*)   My God. And did you go?

Anthony   Yes, I did.]

I stood on that bloody bridge for an hour and a half hoping to see her jump. No such luck. Not so much as a ripple. So I went home again.

[**Henry**   She was on Albert Bridge, actually.

Anthony (*uninterested*)   Was she? Oh well, that figures.]

Anyway, that's beside the point. Karen Knightly is totally immaterial. I've forgotten her. We're talking about Imogen. And that one you can forget. You keep out of my chickens. Away from my cows. Off my pigs. And well clear of my wife, all right?

Scrambled Feet by John Driver and Jeffrey Haddow

John, twenties, American, but any accent (with slight adjustments) would work.

Scrambled Feet is a musical revue on the topic of an actor's life, so all the scenes, sketches and songs depict an aspect of the theatrical experience, such as agents, touring, producers etc. The scenes are unrelated except by theme.

Although not the usual source of good radio monologues, the revue supplies one of the best examples of a speech that can exploit the uniqueness of radio: here is a perfect opportunity to use microphone technique to convey both inner and outer voices of the actor.

This particular monologue, 'No Small Roles', is self-contained. It looks at the pressures encountered by those lowly thespians who have little to contribute to the performance of a play, but have to wait wordlessly onstage for extended periods, supernumeraries who may have trained for years to deliver a couple of unimportant lines that anyone could say.

We hear inside the mind of 'John', playing a spear carrier in *Julius Caesar* one hot summer's night in New York's Central Park. Wearing heavy armour and anxiously anticipating the cue for his one line, John becomes distracted by all the things he can see and hear during the wait.

In the stage version the character 'John' is onstage while 'Jeff' does the voice-over from offstage. Here, the radio actor can do John's voices for himself, the one in his head and the one the theatre audience hears. Using both an intimate inner voice and a more projected one will effectively convey the idea of the piece.

John (*voice-over*)   I can't believe the Romans really wore this stuff, especially in the summer. No wonder they lost the Empire. At least it's nice being here in the park every night. (*Sound of mosquito.*) Oh, God, it's under my breastplate. (*Sound of slurping.*) That's gonna itch. This is my big act, where I have my line. Four years of college and two years of graduate school for one line. Why don't they just shut up and stab him? Everybody knows the story. Look at that Cassius. He's supposed to have a lean and hungry look so they cast a three-hundred-pound Mexican. Here he goes with my favorite line: 'The fawlt dear Brutoos eez not in our starss, but een ourselfs dat we are underwear.' That's what happens when you learn the part phonetically. Uh-oh he's got trouble with his body mike. Can't hear a thing. (*Sound: feedback, buzz, 'Breaker 1-9, Breaker 1-9, I need a traffic report on the . . .' beep.*) No, it's OK. Arrgh, there's the itch and I can't move. What did the director say? (*With fey lisp.*) 'A Centurian never flinches . . .' Is that my cue? Was that my line? No, no, I'm OK. Boooring. 1, 2, 3, 4, 5, 6, etc. . . . 25. There are 25 bald people in the audience. Hey, there's the agent I invited. He's looking at me. Oh, boy, I can see him! Oh, no, I can see him. I forgot to take my glasses off. How could I spend 30 minutes in front of a mirror getting into character and forget to take off my glasses? (*Reaches for them.*) Wait, if I take them off now everyone will notice. Well, what am I worried about? The Romans had glass they had metal. Wait, here comes my line. Here it comes . . . (*Said by **John** onstage.*) Sail Heaser! (*Voice-over.*) Shit, shit, shit, shit, shit! One lousy line and I blew it. (*Sound of mosquito.*) At least I'm working. (*Sound of slurping.*)

Silent Engine by Julian Garner

Bill, thirties, any accent.

This speech forms part of a central monologue in this two-hander about a couple's inability to confront the death of their baby and the reality of their relationship. Bill has been with his wife Anna for fifteen years. They recently had a daughter die ten days after her birth. Neither of them has come to terms with their loss and both are raging and grieving, each in their own way.

An architect by profession – though he's had no paid work for a long time - Bill has been carrying massive debts and has become unable to cope on top of the agony of his daughter's death. During a walking holiday in the West Country, distraught, overcome with his problems and wanting to die, he ran into the sea. Anna saved his life but he went on to have a total breakdown. Here, some time after that breakdown, he recounts with a poignant clarity some of the events that led to it.

The speech comprises two extracts taken from the long monologue by Bill.

Bill The day after the birth, I had to go to London, to discuss my feasibility study for Lambeth; converting an old swimming baths into a community resource centre. I was feeling confident, I'd done a good job, and I had it on good authority that the project had cross-party support, which meant it would probably go through on the nod. I bought a cup of coffee from the trolley. The water, as usual wasn't boiling, so the granules floated on the top like dead ants, but I wasn't going to let that spoil my day. I was a father! I was an architect! This was the first day of the rest of my life! And . . . I had a polaroid of Marion – aged two and half minutes – to gaze at all the way to Charing Cross.

Takes a Polaroid from the wallet.

But when I looked at it . . .

Gazes at it impassively for a moment then holds it up for the audience to see.

I don't know if you can see it from where you are. It was a dud film, the image hadn't fixed. I call it 'Baby Marion in the Fog'. She's in there somewhere, wandering about. Lost.

He puts the Polaroid in his wallet and the wallet in his pocket.

I stayed in the toilet all the way to London. I felt like someone'd stabbed me in the throat. Kept trying to tell myself it didn't matter – I'd been there, hadn't I?

Silence.

[. . .]

Long pause, then fast:

Tenth day, middle of the night, Marion suddenly screaming for no reason, eyes bulging, terrified, we call the doctor, who calls an ambulance, they rush her to hospital, shes's ice-cold, moaning, wrapped in blakets. Anna can't stop her own teeth chattering, not from cold.

At the hospital, they can't raise a vein, no circulation, she's acidotic, it's her heart.

We sit for an hour in the corridor, in the dark, sick children asleep in the wards, Anna shaking. 'What do you think it is? she says. 'Do you think . . . ? What is it? What?!' We hold hands til they sweat, nurses run in and out of the treatment room. At two o'clock, I go in, they've got Marion on a table, tubes sticking out of her neck like a broken telephone.

I cough, and say, 'If the news is bad, I think my wife'll need sedation.' The consultant glances up: 'No, it doesn't look good,' she says. I feel like someone stabs me in the throat. Oh God, please dear God, oh please, please dear God.

Some Girl(s) by Neil LaBute

Man, thirty-three, American accent.

A nameless 'Man' goes on a trip to meet up with a clutch of women to determine which of them he should be with. Each has been deserted by him in the past when he has hooked up with some other girl that's taken his fancy.

This writer/teacher, career progressing nicely, is about to marry, but he has a commitment phobia. He's got cold feet and feels driven to re-visit his ex-girlfriends, just to check that none of them was 'the one'. He aims to apologise for past misdeeds, but also, in furtherance of his writing career, he's made a deal with *Esquire* magazine to secretly record these meetings, for later publication.

Jetting all over America, staying in characterless hotel rooms, so far he's received a bit of a battering – bitterness, anger, incredulousness – but now he's with Bobbi, a ravishing beauty with whom he had a relationship at the age of twenty-three. Suddenly he realises that *she* was the one, and that fact had been his subconscious reason for leaving ten years before.

This speech at the end of the play follows his admission that he once harboured an interest in Bobbi's twin sister – an admission he makes thinking his honesty will be endearing – and then Bobbi's accidental finding of the recording equipment in his jacket. Confessing, proclaiming his conviction that he will never stray again and imploring her to forgive him, he is greeted with derision and anger. She goes to leave but he stops her with one last desperate entreaty for her understanding and forgiveness.

An unsympathetic character, he nevertheless has his genuine – though selfish – motives. He's left a trail of devastation in his wake and he's sharply aware of the feelings in the heart of the listener; even so, he's going for broke.

It's worth bearing in mind that, when Bobbi leaves shortly afterwards, never to return, he immediately calls his fiancée, reverting to type.

Man Bobbi . . . hold on. Please! You have to hear this! *Have to!*

The **Woman** *doesn't verbally agree. She simply stops where she is. Even backs up a touch. He has the floor.*

Look, it's as simple as this: I'm *sorry*. I did a . . . stupid, stupid thing back so many years ago – I could try and place blame on something else, say it's a horrible age we live in now, a world that doesn't give two shits about people's feelings and, and . . . where folks stay up until four in the morning searching for sex on the internet while their partner is sleeping ten feet away! Or some guy will *text-message* his wife to say, 'I'm leaving you.' All these little daily atrocities that we visit on each other that are really pretty breathtaking . . . (*Beat.*) But I can't. That's not the problem. *This* was my fault, all of it. I was just young and, I dunno, goofy and, you know – those were my *good* qualities – I'm a guy, I'm bad at this, Bobbi. I found the single greatest person I could ever imagine being near, I mean *standing* near, even, and she liked me. Me! And that just didn't compute, it did not make sense, no matter what she said to me . . . so I made myself believe it wasn't true and I ran off. Like some two-year-old child would do. (*Beat.*) But I've grown up since then, I have – all this being with other women and writing about it and telling myself that I should go visit my past before I marry . . . it's all about *you*. I don't care if you buy it or hate me or laugh in my face . . . (*Tears up a bit.*) I need you and . . . oh boy. No way I'm gonna top that one, so I'll just leave off right there. I need you, Bobbi. Not your sister, not anybody else I've ever known, even this girl I'm supposed to marry . . . no one. Just you.

The **Man** *stops now and waits – the* **Woman** *doesn't even blink.*

. . . I wish you'd say something.

'Car' from *Street Trilogy* by Chris O'Connell

Gary, thirties, any accent.

Gary has had his car, his pride and joy, stolen and what's worse, when he threw himself into the path of the car and the four young tearaways who were taking it, they compounded his fury by driving straight at him, seriously injuring him. But the damage wasn't just physical – Gary's whole equilibrium has been destroyed.

It's two weeks after the event and one of the lads, Nick, has given himself up. Already on probation, he has been overwhelmed by guilt, worrying that the victim might be dead and that he might go to prison for life. The probation officer, Rob, decides that a mediation session might reconcile the feelings of both victim and perpetrator and, in a call to Gary's home, puts him under some pressure to participate.

All Gary's feelings of terror, anger, humiliation and resentment come flooding back at the thought of coming face to face with the offender, just so that the young criminal can, in Gary's opinion, feel better about what he's done. Outrage threatens to engulf him and he fears his own possible loss of control.

Here, his words come tumbling out in what is a stream-of-consciousness description of the call from Rob that he dreaded so much, and all the conflicting and violent emotions that the call provokes within him. He is alone in his house, talking to himself.

The punctuation here – or lack of it – is of great significance and should not be ignored.

Gary I'm in the bath and the phone rings I can hear the phone ringing and Melanie's out for the night and I know the answer machine's not on so I'm out of the bath and I'm dripping across the landing to the bedroom where I answer the phone and Robert says he hopes he didn't disturb me and I laugh and say of course he didn't and inside I know what he's about to ask me how he's following up this mediation thing he mentioned before it's been in his head and it's been in mine every minute every day and it's going to be his question like I knew it would be and inside I know if I say yes I'll do it it's just so I can get to see the little bastard for the first time the one who nearly killed me but just as I swap hands and put the receiver in my other hand I'm feeling weak like my legs are going to give way because I suddenly think will this mediation stuff make me feel better or worse when I get to set eyes on him and it's going round and round my head again how it's not fair how this has happened to me and I'm getting this sort of phone call and this sort of pressure and how the bubble's burst around me and the world's pouring in but I hear myself speaking and I'm telling Robert I'll do it I'll go to the mediation because I'm a good bloke and I want to be a man and do what a person needs to do and I make him understand it's not just for me it's for everyone who ever got anything nicked and I tell Melanie when she gets in and I've still got the wet towel round me and she says I'll feel better for it . . . (*He stops.*) So, I'm trying not to think about it . . . (*Beat.*) I've been trying not to think about it.

The Sugar Syndrome by Lucy Prebble

Lewis, twenty-two, any accent.

Taking three characters who meet through an Internet chat room, this play tackles tricky subjects such as paedophilia and teenage psychological disorders.

A would-be rock-music critic, actually working in telesales, Lewis has been 'dating' seventeen-year-old Dani. They conducted a fairly explicit affair on screen before meeting. Now, they have met twice, at his place, where having fully indulged his physical appetite and sexual fantasies, he's starting to crave her. However, she is far less engaged on every level and is more curious than excited by their relationship. She has been out of touch for six days now, after fairly consistent communication through chat room and mobile, and this is probably one of many emails he has written but never sent.

The fun in this speech on the microphone is playing with what he is writing, what reading, and what revising, so the tempo and timing of the piece is, by turns, varied and unexpected according to the actor's choice.

Lewis To Dani2752@demon.co.uk, Dani. You absent bitch. I miss you. It's been six days, man. I'm sounding a little bit mental, which I don't like. I rang you again and no answer. I get the feeling you're actively not ringing me now. What if you're dead? How would I ever find out? No one would think to call me. I'd just sit here for ever looking at this screen.

You don't even have to call, you could just email me to tell me why you're not calling. At least then I'd KNOW.

I can't think about anything else, you've taken over my brain. Every part of me is willing that little gold envelope to appear. Send and receive. Send and receive. But when it does it's always nubile young Russian girl-on-girl action. Still.

The clock tells me it is far too late for anyone to be calling anyone. I tell the clock to shut up, what do you know, you're a fucking clock.

I apologise to the clock. It has always been there before when you've written and may be a lucky charm.

I think you're lovely. Sometimes I want to smash your face in, like now, to remind you I'm here, but I think you're lovely. Will you not just write a little? Just to keep me going? Cos I just keep imagining what you could be doing and it's sending me mental. I'm sorry but it is. I miss you. Obviously in a manly, independent, not bothered way. But I do.

He sighs.

Save as draft.

Under the Blue Sky by David Eldridge

Graham, thirty-six, any accent.

Under the Blue Sky tells its story of six interconnected school-teachers in three acts, each featuring one of three couples. The middle act centres on two lonely colleagues from an independent school in Essex, who, desperate for affection, throw themselves at each other, denying to themselves the fundamental dislike they mutually feel.

Graham is a history teacher at the school and also trains the school cadet force. For some time he has been obsessed with Michelle, a sexy but troubled woman in her late thirties. Michelle has often confided in him, luridly describing her sexual exploits, but showing no interest whatsoever in him as a man.

Despite his erotic daydreams, Graham knows that he is out of her league, but it hasn't stopped him hoping. Unexpectedly, Michelle has asked him out, and after a night of excess alcohol and flirting they stumble lecherously back to his place, where his wildest dreams look like coming true. So successful is his arousal that he suffers a premature ejaculation, the sobering effects of which bring an immediate end to their foreplay and initiate a barrage of self loathing and recrimination from Michelle, in which she also heartlessly ridicules him and everything he stands for, particularly his military-style bullying of pupils.

Stung by the shocking vitriol of her condemnation, embarrassed by his failure and empowered by the lack of restraint that *she* has shown, he finally plucks up the courage to stand up for himself and in this response he lets go of his feelings with a new abandonment, pointing out her questionable behaviour, hoping to hurt her to the same degree. He's always been scared of Michelle, but now that he sees her for what she is, he's able to unburden himself freely, even though as he relates how he's been stalking her, he exposes his own creepy behaviour.

Graham *throws more flowers at her.*

Graham I got them for you!

A slight pause.

I went to the high street at lunchtime and I got them for you. After dinner. A Chinese meal. Back here. I'd give them to you. And you would like them. And be delighted and happy. That there were such beautiful flowers. For you.

He throws more flowers at her and throws the bouquet on the floor. He stamps on the bouquet and kicks it.

You go on and on and on about me but who are you? You're just a selfish cow. You've been at the school seven years and you still haven't even got your own form. You never get involved with anything or anyone. You're just interested in drawing your salary and your sordid succession of men.

[**Michelle** Which you wank yourself silly over . . .]

Graham And the theatre club? You only do that so you can pour out your disgusting mind to me and to try and appear cultured at school. You're the only person I know who thought that teacher in the play with Michael Gambon was accurate! You don't care about anything. You don't know anything. You have a mind that connects with numbers and that is about it because you certainly have no soul!

A slight pause.

I'm a man, a man. Although I don't feel much like one sometimes!

Acknowledgements

p. 76   Extract from *The Revengers' Comedies* by Alan Ayckbourn (Faber & Faber Ltd). Copyright © 1991 Alan Ayckbourn. Reproduced by permission of Faber & Faber Ltd. Performance rights: Casarotto Ramsay & Associates Ltd, London (www.casarotto.uk.com) [professional] / Samuel French Ltd (www.samuelfrench-london.co.uk) [amateur]

p. 62   Extract from *No End of Blame* by Howard Barker (Calder Publications). Copyright © 1981 Howard Barker. Reproduced by permission of Calder Publications Ltd. Performance rights: Judy Daish Associates Ltd, 2 St Charles Place, London, W10 6EG

p. 46   Extract from *Girl, Watching* by Jyll Bradley (Oberon Books). Copyright © 2003 Jyll Bradley. Reproduced by permission of Oberon Books Ltd. Performance rights: PFD (www.pfd.co.uk)

p. 48   Extract from *Kiss Me Like You Mean It* by Chris Chibnall (Oberon Books). Copyright © 2001 Chris Chibnall. Reproduced by permission of Oberon Books Ltd. Performance rights: ICM, 76 Oxford Street, London [professional] / Samuel French Ltd (www.samuelfrench-london.co.uk) [amateur]

p. 38   Extract from *Flush* by David Dipper (Nick Hern Books). Copyright © 2004 David Dipper. Reproduced by permission of Nick Hern Books Ltd (www.nickhernbooks.co.uk). Performance rights: Nick Hern Books Ltd (info@nickhernbooks.demon.co.uk) [amateur]

p. 18   Extract from *Bone* by John Donnelly (Faber & Faber Ltd). Copyright © 2004 John Donnelly. Reproduced by permission of Faber & Faber Ltd. Performance rights: Alan Brodie Representation Ltd (www.alanbrodie.com)

(originally commissioned and broadcast by BBC Radio 4).
Copyright © 2005 Katie Hims. Reproduced by permission of
Ms K Hims and BBC Radio 4. Performance rights:
please contact Methuen Drama in the first instance with
details of your performance plans (all performance rights
enquiries will be forwarded to the author)

p. 26 Extract from *Digging for Fire* by Declan Hughes from *Plays 1*
(Methuen Drama). Copyright © 1993 Declan Hughes.
Performance rights: ICM, 76 Oxford Street, London

p. 64 Extract from *Osama the Hero* by Dennis Kelly (Oberon Books).
Copyright © 2005 Dennis Kelly. Reproduced by permission of
Oberon Books Ltd. Performance rights: Casarotto Ramsay &
Associates Ltd (www.casarotto.uk.com)

p. 20 Extract from *Borderline* by Hanif Kureshi (Calder
Publications). Copyright © 1981 Hanif Kureshi. Reproduced
by permission of Calder Publications Ltd. Performance rights:
The Agency (info@theagency.co.uk)

p. 84 Extract from *Some Girls* by Neil La Bute (Faber & Faber Ltd).
Copyright © 2005 Neil La Bute. Reproduced by permission of
Faber & Faber Ltd. Performance rights: please contact Faber &
Faber Ltd in the first instance (www.faber.co.uk)

p. 40 Extract from *Frozen* by Bryony Lavery (Faber & Faber Ltd).
Copyright © Bryony Lavery. Reproduced by permission of
Faber & Faber Ltd. Performance rights: PFD (www.pfd.co.uk)
[professional] / Samuel French Ltd (www.samuelfrench-
london.co.uk) [amateur]

p. 68 Extract from *Our Bad Magnet* by Douglas Maxwell (Oberon
Books). Copyright © 2001 Douglas Maxwell. Reproduced by
permission of Oberon Books Ltd. Performance rights: PFD
(www.pfd.co.uk)

p. 50 Extract from *The Lieutenant of Inishmore* by Martin McDonagh
(Methuen Drama). Copyright © 2001 Martin McDonagh.

by permission of Oberon Books Ltd. Performance rights: PFD (www.pfd.co.uk)

p. 88   Extract from *The Sugar Syndrome* by Lucy Prebble (Methuen Drama). Copyright © 2003 Lucy Prebble. Performance rights: The Rod Hall Agency (www.rodhallagency.com) [professional] / Samuel French Ltd (www.samuelfrench-london.co.uk) [amateur]

p. 36   Extract from *Five Kinds of Silence* by Shelagh Stephenson from *Plays 1* (Methuen Drama) Copyright © 1997, 2003 Shelagh Stephenson. Reproduced by permission of Methuen Drama. Performance rights: Julia Tyrrell Management Ltd, 57 Greenham Road, London, N10 1LN (julia@jtmanagement.co.uk)

p. 54   Extract from *Lovers and Other Strangers* by Renée Taylor & Joseph Bologna. Copyright © 1968 Renée Taylor & Joseph Bologna. Performance rights: Samuel French Inc., US (www.samuelfrench.com)

p. 28   Extract from *Divine Right* by Peter Whelan (Warner Chappell Plays). Copyright © 1996 Peter Whelan. Reproduced by permission of The Agency (London) Ltd, 24 Pottery Lane, London, W11 4LZ. Performance rights: The Agency (London) Ltd (info@theagency.co.uk) [professional] / Josef Weinberger Ltd (www.josef-weinberger.com) [amateur]

p. 52   Extract from *Little Sweet Thing* by Roy Williams (Methuen Drama). Copyright © 2005 Roy Williams. Reproduced by permission of Methuen Drama. Performance rights: Alan Brodie Representation Ltd (www.alanbrodie.com)

p. 70   Extract from *Peepshow* by Isabel Wright (Oberon Books). Copyright © 2003 Isabel Wright. Reproduced by permission of Oberon Books Ltd. Performance rights: PFD (www.pfd.co.uk)

p. 34   Extract from *Dogs Barking* by Richard Zajdlic (Faber & Faber

Ltd). Copyright © 1999 Richard Zajdlic. Reproduced by
permission of Faber & Faber Ltd. Performance rights: PFD
(www.pfd.co.uk)

p. 44 Extract from *Germinal* by Émile Zola (translated by William
Gaminara). Copyright © 1988 William Gaminara.
Reproduced by permission of Oberon Books Ltd. Performance
rights: The Agency (London) Ltd (info@theagency.co.uk)
[professional] / Samuel French Ltd (www.samuelfrench-
london.co.uk) [amateur]

Disclaimer

Caution Notice